Choose Life Journal:

A Transformational Journey with the Word & Spirit

BY:

ROLLAND WRIGHT

I am writing you on behalf of my personal experience with the Transformative Journal Plan for Personal Bible Study.

Through this journaling system I have seen my own walk deepen with the Lord, in applying these principles set forth.

In this process it has led me to meditate on the Scriptures and has opened a pathway to ask, listen, and then ponder what the Spirit is communicating with me.

In the application of using this method my walk has been strengthened in the application of the Word!

Taking the step to journal what the Lord is saying and take it before the Lord in prayer has been a powerful tool to be attentive to the leading of the Spirit in understanding and applying God's Word to my life.

The worship music has been a beautiful way to bring the message home and to touch my heart in yet a deeper place.

I am excited to begin to apply the daily mentoring of Choose Life.

God has brought forth a timely and powerful tool to instruct His bride. A mentorship of deepening the understanding and application of God's Word, transforming the lives of the one seeking a deeper and more intimate walk with Jesus. For His Glory,

Deborah Wick

Having been a Chaplain for First Responders and Hospice, stress can be very hard at times. I have learned through daily journaling to tap into God's love, power, and counsel. The act of sitting with Him and listening to the Spirit, has changed my life. Choose Life is a great tool to use to help me daily stay on track. I highly endorse the Choose Life program and suggest you download the phone app, like I did. You will be pleased at the life change it will bring you.

Chaplain Caliatra McIndoo

All man knows about God has come from His revelation about Himself. That revelation has been disclosed through His written Word. This reality has been a catalyst in my life to focus daily on reading, studying. and applying the Word of God. The plan the author shares has been a tool to help me grow in my faith by becoming a more sincere and effective follower of Christ. This daily discipline reminds me I can trust God with all my life and depend on him for everything. The daily process outlined has been transformative by encouraging, guiding, and correcting me when I have needed it. It has trained my heart and mind to become more humble, kind, and faithful. Daily reading and applying God's Word through a daily action statement has taught me to hear God's voice, understand His will for my life, help me feel close to God and have a constant assurance that I am never alone. Following the principles outlined in *Choose Life Journal: A transformational journey with the Word & Spirit* will release your own personal journey.

Rick McGregor

Published by:
Wright Publishing Company - Everett WA
Website: www.FirstPlaceMinistries.com
Email: Rolland@FirstPlaceMinistries.com

Copyright Use and Public Information
Unless otherwise noted, images have been used according to public information laws.

ISBN: 979-8-218-04875-4 Paperback

Limits of Liability and Disclaimer of Warranty: The author and publisher shall not be liable for the reader's misuse of this material. This book is strictly for informational and education purposes.

Unless otherwise noted, Scriptures taken from the Tree of Life version

©2015 by theMessianic Jewish Family Bible Society.

"TLV" and "Tree of LIfe Version" and "Tree of Life Holy Scriptures" are trademarks registered in the United States Patent and Trademark office by the Messianic Family Bible Society.

Disclaimer:
The views expressed are those of the author and do not reflect the official policy or position of the publisher or First Place Ministries. This publication is designed to provide accurate and authoritative information regarding the subject matter covered. It is sold with the understanding that the publisher is not engaged in rendering legal, accounting, clinical or other preofessional advice. If legal advice or other expert assistance is required, the services of a competent professional should be sought. The opinions expressed by the authors of this book are not endorsed by First Place Ministries, and are the sole responsibility of the author rendering the opinion.

Choose Life Journal

A TRANSFORMATIONAL JOURNEY
WITH THE WORD & SPIRIT
BY
ROLLAND WRIGHT

DEDICATION

What a privilege to dedicate this book to my children,

Christopher Adam Wright,

Jennifer Anne Ross, and

Bethany Lee Wright.

It was really for them and their children and their children's children, that I began journaling. I wanted to leave something behind which would be a guide to their discovering God and a relationship which I have enjoyed for years. It is a sobering reality that I cannot choose a relationship with God for them, any more than King David or the prophet Samuel could.

It is a fascinating journey to be processed and transformed by the Holy Spirit. I find it interesting how the Holy Spirit has led me to select Deuteronomy 30 as the name and basis for this book. Chris, Jennifer, and Bethany, I pray for you daily.

"I call the heavens and the earth to witness about you today, that I have set before you life and death, the blessing and the curse. Therefore, Choose Life so that you and our descendants may live, by loving Adonai your God, listening to His voice, and clinging to Him. For He is your life and the length of your days." Deuteronomy 30:19-20a

Heirloom platter belonging to
Marcella Wright, grandmother of
Christopher, Jennifer, and Bethany.

Acknowledgements

I want to begin with celebrating my parents, Herman & Marcella Wright, for seventy years of marriage this past June '22. You both are a model of constancy in marriage and faith.

I want to thank Jackie Morey, who helped to launch the first of several books in 2017. I never anticipated there were more books to be written any more than I have any awareness that there are more books beyond this one.

It is a fascinating process how the Holy Spirit brings people in and out of one's life. I met Joe Monroe in the mid to late 90's through working together for an area painting contractor. He re-enters my life a couple of months prior to the great lock down in 2020, in pain and facing the loss of a long-term, 30+ year marriage.

Solomon claims that *"As iron sharpens iron, so a person sharpens the countenance of his friend"* Proverbs 27:7.

I have been privileged to walk with Joe through this season of loss and career change. I hope we have sharpened each other. Thank you for adding a global, missional testimony of your experience years ago as a college student. Even in the face of governmental suppression, truth is sought and embraced.

I met my cousin Rita as a child. Her mother is my maternal grandmother's sister. Her father was the produce manager at the local grocery store my family shopped at. I remember Uncle Dale fondly. Interesting how we have been separated geographically for most of our lives, yet we have reunited in faith and spirit over the past couple of years, praying weekly for our children and grandchildren. Thank you, Rita, for your prayerful and financial support. It is not overlooked and is graciously appreciated.

A huge shoutout to those who receive my daily Choose Life Journal and engage with me in the daily process. I pray and wish for you the transformation which I see and experience in my life because of sitting before the Holy Spirit, allowing Him to reconcile, renew, repurpose, refresh, redirect, reorganize, and restore that which is broken. He is the mentor of all mentors. One touch and you will never be the same. He will lead you and guide you into all truth. He is the King of all Kings and the Lord of all Lords.

I want to thank my Ekklesia community for their support. Our community is ever expanding and growing as each of us embrace our individual callings and giftings in the kingdom of God. Thank you for being a community of active doing and vigilant faith. Thank you for being a voice of one crying in the wilderness and a light to the world.

I want to thank Kristi Knowles, my virtual assistant and editor for this project. Kristi has taken on multiple tasks for First Place Ministries including website content changes, the electronic requirements of daily journal entries, a monthly newsletter, and the addition of the Choose Life Journal phone app. All components combine to make what we do possible. Kristi is a key contributor to the success of First Place Ministries. I could not do this without you.

TABLE OF CONTENTS

Choose Life Journal

A TRANSFORMATIONAL JOURNEY
WITH THE WORD & SPIRIT
BY:
Rolland Wright

INTRODUCTION

I want to assert from the beginning why I am authoring this book. When you find something which has transformed your life, you want to share it with everyone.

Case in point, I lost almost thirty-five pounds a couple of years ago. A friend introduced me to a system which had helped her shed twice the weight I was looking to lose. I saw her before and after pictures and believed it would work for me too, and it did. I started the program in April and by September 1st, I had shed the weight. I had the discipline to stay the plan, and 1.5 to 2 pounds were dropped each week. She was my accountability coach, and I knew my "why" - I wanted to avoid the later in life diseases which run in my family, and I wanted to feel better. My weight had climbed at one pound per year which doesn't sound like much. But, when you are approaching fifty years since your High School graduation, it means you are fifty pounds heavier than when you graduated.

Being overweight was no longer acceptable. When friends see results, they ask you how you did it. When others see success, they don't hesitate to ask you, "How did you do it?"

Similarly, our spiritual life mirrors our physical life. I have developed a Bible journaling plan based on the transformation of my relationship with God.

If you are tired of wandering through life aimlessly, I challenge you to not only read this book, but apply the principles of the Choose Life Bible Journaling plan.

You see, I am a product of the product. I used a similar system for over 15 years, modified it, personalized it, customized it, and created a new system with more options. Anyone who can read and write can do this plan. From the newly born again, to the one who is a seared veteran of the Bible, and to everyone in-between, a daily discipline of coming to the Word can be established. You must come hungry, curious, intentional, self-disciplined, and teachable. This plan relies on the Holy Spirit doing the mentoring and your commitment to persevering every day, sitting at the Holy Spirit's feet. Make an appointment every day, at the same time, which is un-cancelable, non-negotiable, and sealed in stone.

My experience:

> *When I show up, God shows up! and,*
> *When I get into His Word, His Word gets into me!*

God promises, "*Draw near to Me (God), and I (He) will draw near to you" (Jacob/James 4:8).* If I do my part, God will do His.

God declares to us through Jeremiah:

> *Then you will call on Me, and come and pray to Me, and I will listen to you. You will seek Me and find Me, when you will search for Me with all your heart. Then I will be found by you," says Adonai, "and I will return you from exile, and gather you from all the nations and from all the places where I have driven you, "says Adonai, "and I will bring you back to the place from which I removed you as captives into exile (Jeremiah 29:13-14).*

How much of my heart does Adonai ask for? How much of our hearts does he require? All! He wants "all" of my heart. The New Testament Covenant which Jesus declared says,

> *You shall love Adonai your God with all your heart, and with all your soul, and with all your strength, and with all your mind, and your neighbor as yourself (Luke 10:27 & Mark 12:30).*

How much again does God want? All of me. All of my heart, my soul, my strength, my mind.

How much does He require? All.

How much am I giving Him? Again, I ask myself and you, how much does He require? *All.*

You may be trying to define the word *all*. How much does *all* mean? Until we resolve the amount within us, we certainly won't give Him our all. We have the capacity to deceive ourselves and be deceived, but the requirement is not diminished. He wants all our hearts, minds, and souls. Let's get busy working toward His standard and not ours.

There are three things which I began to request of God.

First, I wanted more of the Holy Spirit, not less, more. When I read the end of Mark 16, I read these words:

> *These signs will accompany those who believe:*
> *In My name they will drive out demons,*

they will speak new languages;
they will handle snakes;
and if they drink anything deadly, it will not harm them;
they will lay hands on the sick, and they will get well
(vs 17-18).

Why did I want more of the Holy Spirit? Because I wanted to see and experience the "signs" that will "accompany those who believe!" I was tired and through with not experiencing and seeing the *power* which was displayed by the early community of faith! It was *power* which was poured out upon them in Acts 1:8,

*"But you will receive **power** when the Ruach ha-Kodesh has come upon you; and you will be my witnesses."*

It was power given by the Holy Spirit when Peter and John healed a lame man at Solomon's Portico of which they testified:

*"Why do you stare at us—as if by our own **power** or godliness we had made this man walk? This demonstration of power befuddled "the kohanim and the captain of the Temple and the Sadducees" (4:1),*

but it led to "about five thousand" believing the message of "Yeshua (and) the resurrection of the dead" (4:2).

The next day:

"the rulers and elders and Torah scholars were gathered together in Jerusalem. Annas the kohen-gadol was there, and Caiaphas and John and Alexander, and all those who were of high-priestly descent. When they had placed Peter and John in their midst, they began to inquire, "By what power or in what name did you do this?" (4:7)

Our power source is the same today, yesterday and forever. Amen! So, where is the disconnect? Are we laying hands on the sick and evidencing healings in the power of the Holy Spirit? Are we casting out demons? Are we seeing the accompanying signs of those who believe?

The sad thing is, we are told in the end times that God will pour out His Spirit. Listen to these words found in Joel 3:1-5 and repeated in Acts 2:17-21.

[17] 'And it shall be in the last days,' says God, 'that I will pour out My Ruach on all flesh. Your sons and your daughters shall prophesy, your young men shall see visions, and your

old men shall dream dreams. [18] Even on My slaves, male and female, I will pour out My Ruach in those days, and they shall prophesy. [19] And I will give wonders in the sky above and signs on the earth beneath—blood, and fire, and smoky vapor. [20] The sun shall be turned to darkness and the moon to blood before the great and glorious Day of ADONAI comes. [21] And it shall be that everyone who calls on the name of ADONAI shall be saved.

These passages are declarations of God! *"I will (do) pour out my Ruach (Spirit)."* Do you hear it, and do you receive it? I am believing God for this promise because, in Malachi 3:23-24 he records this message from God:

[23] "Behold, I am going to send you Elijah the prophet, before the coming of the great and terrible day of ADONAI. [24] He will turn the hearts of fathers to the children, and the hearts of children to their fathers—else I will come and strike the land with utter destruction."

Secondly, I want to experience with other followers of Messiah, the dynamic of the early faith community recorded and documented by Luke in Acts 2:42-47

[42] They were devoting themselves to the teaching of the emissaries and to fellowship, to breaking bread and to prayers. [43] Fear lay upon every soul, and many wonders and signs were happening through the emissaries. [44] And all who believed were together, having everything in common. [45] They began selling their property and possessions and sharing them with all, as any had need. [46] Day by day they continued with one mind, spending time at the Temple and breaking bread from house to house. They were sharing meals with gladness and sincerity of heart, [47] praising God and having favor with all the people. And every day the Lord was adding to their number those being saved.

I am not seeking utopia, nor am I proposing we try to regain entrance to the Garden of Eden, but I am of the mind that we can return to the mindset and heart of the early community of faith who were "devoting" themselves to the apostles (emissaries) teaching and fellowship. Most of us have not experienced the type of home-to-home fellowship they experienced, and we are forfeiting a vital element of community by not engaging in this model.

I define this early community of faith model as the working definition of Ekklesia.

If you are not familiar with the term Ekklesia, my fourth published book, ***Ekklesia Declared!***, provides you with historical information about the transition of Ekklesia to the word "church," in translations dating back to the King James version. If you want a greater understanding of the transition and the implications for all followers of Jesus, books are available for purchase through *www.firstplaceministries.com* or on Amazon.

Additionally, the early community of faith possessed a unity which I have not witnessed or experienced. I have seen and experienced great expressions of generosity, but this Acts community demonstrated "commonism" as a whole heart and mind set. No, I did not say communism or socialism. Both of those philosophies are forced or mandated. The "commonism" Luke documents is voluntary. It is a heart condition and a lifestyle. It was characterized by everyone when they *"began selling their property and possessions and sharing them with all, as anyone had need"* (Acts 2:45).

This is not the heart and mind-set of America nor of the world. This is the mindset of a transformed heart and mind under the influence of the Holy Spirit. To get back to an Acts community of faith Spirit-controlled lifestyle requires a fully transformed heart and mind. Where do we see this philosophy mentioned?

In Romans 12:1-2, Paul writes these words.

> *I urge you (could be translated "implore you with a strong urgency!") therefore, brothers and sisters, (with no bias between genders, equally inclusive), by the mercies of God, to present your bodies as a living sacrifice—holy, acceptable to God—which is your spiritual service. Do not be conformed to this world but be transformed by the renewing of your mind, so that you may discern what is the will of God—what is good and acceptable and perfect.*

Transformation is critically important. Transformation precedes knowing or discerning the will of God. I floundered for most of my life until the transformation process, the work of the Holy Spirit, took form in my life. How did that transformation come or happen? Through the Word of God in combination with the Holy Spirit! Period. The Holy Spirit is credited with inspiring the men who wrote or penned the Bible. They were inspired by the Holy Spirit. Likewise, it is the Holy Spirit who indwells those who have had the Acts 2 anointing of the Holy Spirit. Without the Holy Spirit we are powerless. The common denominator of the early faith community was Holy Spirit anointed power which was evidenced by speaking in tongues, casting out demons, laying hands on the sick and healing them, and scores of people testifying of the resurrection of Jesus.

Until we get back to the Holy Spirit anointing which this community experienced, we will not see the evidence(s) which God claimed we would see in the later days. Are we in the later days? If we aren't, it sure feels like it. If it is the end of times, is it applicable to "Do business until I, (Jesus) come back." (Luke 19:13)? This was Jesus' demand regarding the parable of the nobleman who entrusted ten slaves with minding his kingdom while he was away. What is our kingdom assignment? What is our declared identity? Do I have a responsibility to Jesus and His kingdom?

Lastly, I have asked for the fulfillment of Malachi 3:23-24 and Luke 1:17 in my life and my dad's life before we exit this world. You see, both of us have experienced the pain of having a son announce to us they no longer want to associate with us or be a part of the family. I do not wish this on any parent or any father. To be hated by your own flesh and blood is cruel. But we need not be surprised by the rise in fractured families.

As a student of the Bible, I am amazed at the foresight of God to include insight into future events. We are in an era and approaching a time in which we would do well to look at the Scriptures which address the approaching dynamic families will face.

> **Luke 21:16:** *But you will be handed over even by parents, brothers, relatives, and friends—and they will put some of you to death.*

> **Matthew 10:21:** *Brother will betray brother to death, and a father his child; and children will rise up against their parents and have them put to death.*

> **Matthew 10:35-36:** *[35] For I have come to set 'a man against his father, a daughter against her mother, and a daughter-in-law against her mother-in-law; [36] and a man's enemies will be the members of his household.*

> **Mark 13:12-13:** *[12] Brother will betray brother to death, and a father his child. And children will rise up against parents and have them put to death. [13] And you will be hated by all because of My name, but the one who endures to the end will be saved.*

> **Micah 7:6:** *For son treats father with contempt; daughter*

rises up against mother; daughter-in-law against mother-in-law: a man's enemies are the people of his own house.

There are more Scriptures I could emphasize but you get the picture. It is going to get ugly. Notice, that Jesus did not say, "This might happen." *The facture of family relationships is one of the signs of the end times.*

This is a cross cultural, non-racial, bi-partisan phenomenon which will be characteristic of the end times.

I am of the mind that no one will be exempt, but praise God if you are one of the families who avoid this horror. I have seen few families over my years who functioned together in harmony and didn't self-destruct because of jealousies, hatred, sibling rivalry, all conditions of the heart. See the patriarch of a family pass away and you begin to see the true motives and character of the hearts appear.

This is another good reason to study the Bible. The Old Testament is full of examples of dysfunctional families. We can learn a lot about our families and ourselves.

Here is the difficult truth of Scripture which we need to embrace. Jesus gave us a statement in Luke 14:26, which is difficult to swallow,

"If anyone comes to Me and does not hate his own father, mother, wife, children, brothers, and sisters—and yes, even his own life—he cannot be My disciple."

Could Jesus really mean this? Certainly, we love our own flesh and blood. Here in lies the problem. We love our "own" flesh and Jesus is drawing a comparison with *flesh and spirit.*

We have the example and words of Jesus, also documented by Matthew, Mark, and Luke, in which, on an occasion, He was told that His mother and brothers were standing outside. His reply is telling. *"My mother and My brothers are these who are hearing the Word of God and doing it."* He was telling those who were following Him, you are my new spiritual family. You are a part of a new spiritual family once you become born again. While you still have a biological, physical family, you have transitioned to a new spiritual family.

There is a time coming when you will need to embrace your new identity and the family you have now entered relationship with, as members of Ekklesia. If you claim to be His, you need to make the paradigm shift from the physical flesh association and identify with your new spiritual identity.

The time of polarization is here. We are being forced to declare which side we are on. If you identify with Jesus, your allegiance is already decided, and your family may not choose to come with you. Be prepared. This is a harsh reality and because of love of family, you may need to leave loved ones behind. Do we love God with our "all," our everything? Do we love our own life? Are we prepared to pay the price of following Jesus, like most of His disciples did? If following Jesus cost you your career, would you follow Him? If following Jesus cost you your home, would you follow Him? If following Jesus cost you your family, would you follow Him? The cost is high. Will you follow Him?

There is hope. I pray for my children every day. I pray that somehow, God will open their eyes and hearts to Him. I pray that He will send someone who will influence them for the kingdom, and I pray for that I will see manifest in my children the promise found in Malachi and Luke.

What is the promise of God contained in both of the following passages?

> *"Behold, I am going to send you Elijah the prophet, before the coming of the great and terrible day of Adonai. He will turn the hearts of the fathers to the children, and the hearts of the children to their fathers—else I will come and strike the land with utter destruction"* (Malachi 3:23-24).

> *"And he (John the Immerser) will go before Him in the spirit and power of Elijah, to turn the hearts of the fathers to the children and the disobedient ones to the wisdom of the righteous, to make ready for Adonai a prepared people"* (Luke 1:17).

God is going to cause a transformation of heart between fathers and their children. He has promised this change of heart or else, He will *"come and strike the land with utter (complete) destruction."* That is a promise with consequences if not fulfilled.

My father and I have both experienced one of our children withdrawing all connection with the family. Disowning their family. My brother announced to the family years ago that he was born into the wrong family. God gave him the wrong parents, wrong brother, and sisters. He contacts our mother rarely. My son I have not seen in 20 years. When he withdrew from me, he completely isolated me from his daughters, my granddaughters.

This is extremely painful for me, and I am sure, also for my parents. They never talk about it, and I ask occasionally about his welfare. I pray daily for my brother and my son and have asked that both my dad and I will experience reconciliation of our sons before our deaths.

My greatest why (reason) for journaling is the hope, that like the Bible (God's love letter to us), they might someday find my journal (my love letter to them) and hear my heart for them and for God. That somehow, they will develop a relationship with God because of my influence. That they will see the difference between God and religion. That they will feel my love for them and forgive me for the things they have suffered from the divorce with their mother. That they will discover they received a lot of disinformation as children. That there is a spiritual battle for their souls which has been going on for years. I pray they recognize and acknowledge they are loved and have been prayed for, for years by caring grandparents.

God has been so good to me. Between 2015 and 2018, I had the privilege of traveling to Portugal five times and spent a couple summers vacationing there. Each time I visited Portugal, I had opportunities to minister the Word, counsel, fellowship, and teach the journaling concept. In conversations with the local faith community, one thing I found in common was the number of families who were experiencing the disenfranchisement of one of their children or family members. This was an awakening to the realization that I was not alone.

I have discovered, in the Word, that we need not be surprised by the rise and pervasiveness of disenfranchisement in families around the world. This phenomenon is prophesied in Scripture. In Matthew 10:21-22, Jesus is giving instructions to the Twelve as He sends them out. Let's listen in as He says,

> *21 Brother will betray brother to death, and a father his child; and children will rise up against their parents and have them put to death. 22 And you will be hated by all because of My name, but the one who endures to the end shall be saved.*

Similar wording is recorded of Jesus in the same discourse, verses later He says,

> *34 "Do not think that I came to bring shalom on the earth; I did not come to bring shalom, but a sword. 35 For I have come to set*
>
> *'a man against his father, a daughter against her mother, and a daughter-in-law against her mother-in-law; 36 and a man's enemies will be the members of his household.'*

[37] *"He who loves father or mother more than Me isn't worthy of Me, and he who loves son or daughter more than Me isn't worthy of Me. [38] And whoever does not take up his cross and follow after Me isn't worthy of Me. [39] He who finds his life will lose it, and he who loses his life for My sake will find it.*

This may be the same discourse by Jesus and recorded by Luke in 12:49-53.

[49] "I came to pour out fire on the earth, and how I wish it were already ablaze! [50] But I have an immersion to endure, and how distressed I am until it is finished!

[51] "Do you suppose that I have come to bring shalom on earth? No, I tell you, but rather division. [52] From now on there will be five in one house in opposition, three against two and two against three. [53] They will be divided, father against son and son against father,

mother against daughter and daughter against mother,

mother-in-law against daughter-in-law and daughter-in-law against mother-in-law."

The final Scripture I would like to bring to your attention which supports Jesus' instruction to the Twelve, is found in instructions given to a young Timothy by Paul in 2 Timothy 3:1-5:

But understand this, that in the last days hard times will come— [2] for people will be lovers of self, lovers of money, boastful, arrogant, blasphemers, disobedient to parents, ungrateful, unholy, [3] hardhearted, unforgiving, backbiting, without self-control, brutal, hating what is good, [4] treacherous, reckless, conceited, lovers of pleasure rather than lovers of God, [5] holding to an outward form of godliness but denying its power. Avoid these people!

Do you get the picture? We are in a spiritual battle with our family members. Even though the chaos and vitriol are coming from our loved ones, it is not them we are battling with, but with the demonic influences of this world. The chaos will manifest in self obsession, addictions, impulsive behavior, foul language, arrogance, complete disregard for authority including legal and parental, ungratefulness, lack of self-control, hating what is good (yes, haters will call us haters because Scripture disapproves of their lifestyle), hard heartedness, brutality, recklessness, conceit, and holding to a form of godliness but denying its power. What does this passage say for anyone to do if they cross paths with anyone who has this description or lifestyle? It says, "avoid these people!" Why? Because they are toxic and will destroy you. Unless you are willing to cast the demon out of them, I suggest we take Paul's advice.

We are all in danger of demonic influence. I will give you an example. In Mark 5 we see a demoniac who lives in a graveyard, amongst the tombs. He is described as strong and naked, and "night and day, ... he kept screaming and gashing himself with stones." He was tormented by demons 24/7. The man was a "cutter" and a "screamer."

I used to drive school bus for a local school district. I had an elementary route, and the bus was full. Most of the kids were very respectful and behaved well on the bus. However, inevitably, you will have one or two which must act out and usually they sit in the very back of the bus. I was driving a 40-foot bus with 26 seats and a capacity of approximately 52 with two to a seat. This one particular day I had a screamer. It was not constant, but frequently she continued to test the boundaries. I used my microphone to request that whoever was screaming to please stop. It was an annoying and high-pitched scream which little girls are quite skilled at. Well, it didn't stop, in fact, it increased. So, I pulled off the road at the nearest county transit (CT) stop, set my maxi brake, shut the engine off, put the keys in my pocket and walked to the back of the bus. The bus got incredibly quiet, but I was committed to putting this screaming down for good. So, I asked the group of girls sitting in the back, who the guilty party was. They were all hesitant to say anything. So, I asked them collectively to point out the guilty party. Almost like this event was choreographed, they all pointed to one girl. She immediately became defiant and started yelling, "I didn't do it!" I said, "Well, popular opinion says you did!" So, I invited her up to sit close to me for a few days. I gave her a designated seat!

I climbed back in my seat, belted up, turned the engine on and was about to put the bus into gear and release the maxi, when she again protested, "I didn't do it!" and then she screamed! I started laughing and said to her, "That is the same scream that I heard!" The look on her face was priceless. She knew she was busted. She incriminated herself. She never screamed again.

I am not intimating that this little girl was demonically influenced. She had a moment of rebellion, and she was confronted.

Jesus confronted the demons, and the man was released. Notice the contrast of behavior once Jesus sets him free. We are told that the man *was sitting there, dressed in clothes and in his right mind"* (Mark 5:15b). There is solitude and peace. This man was now able to

15

exercise self-control over screaming and cutting himself. He was no longer self-destructive and no longer a menace to the neighboring townspeople. As a side note, however, the swine which the demons entered were immediately suicidal and driven to self-destruction. Some farmer's pig stock was wiped out in minutes, completely destroyed.

I want to add a New Testament reference on the issue of demonic influence and rebellion. In Galatians 5:16-26, Paul is contrasting the battle which goes on between the Ruach (Spirit) and flesh. It is a battle which we all experience. Please read this passage a couple times. First for an overview, and then, read it for making observations about what instruction, what point, Paul is communicating.

> *16 But I say, walk by the Ruach, and you will not carry out the desires of the flesh. 17 For the flesh sets its desire against the Ruach, but the Ruach sets its desire against the flesh—for these are in opposition to one another, so that you cannot do what you want. 18 But if you are led by the Ruach, you are not under law. 19 Now the deeds of the flesh are clear: sexual immorality, impurity, indecency, 20 idolatry, witchcraft, hostility, strife, jealousy, rage, selfish ambition, dissension, factions, 21 envy, drunkenness, carousing, and things like these. I am warning you, just as I warned you before, that those who do such things will not inherit God's kingdom. 22 But the fruit of the Ruach is love, joy, peace, patience, kindness, goodness, faithfulness, 23 gentleness, and self-control—against such things there is no law. 24 Now those who belong to Messiah have crucified the flesh with its passions and desires.*

> *25 If we live by the Ruach, let us also walk by the Ruach. 26 Let us not become conceited—provoking one another, envying one another.*

Notice, Paul makes all kinds of varieties of acting out, influenced by the flesh. There is one word centered in the middle of this list which pops off the page to me, "witchcraft." In the Old Testament, the prophet Samuel is confronting Saul about a battle in which he did not obey Adonai's orders which were given to him by Samuel. The order was to kill everything including the animals, and his soldiers kept some of the booty and animals for themselves. Saul tried to fabricate a lie to Samuel about the animals being kept for sacrificial purposes. Samuel knew that was a lie and that Saul's disobedience was insubordination to God's command. His response to Saul:

Does Adonai delight in burnt offerings and sacrifices as in obeying the voice of Adonai? Behold, to obey is better than sacrifice, to pay heed than the fat of rams. For rebellion is like the sin of divination and stubbornness is like iniquity and idolatry. Since you have rejected Adonai's Word, He has also rejected you as king (1 Samuel 15:22-23).

Samuel called Saul's rebellion equivalent to the "sin of divination" or "witchcraft." Rebellion is an attitude. Rebellion was the sin of Lucifer when he fell from the heavens. Rebellion is a serious character flaw. We tend to think it is "cute" for a two-year-old but beware, God calls it sin and its source is demonic.

FOR GROUP DISCUSSION

1. What is your "why" for developing a daily lifestyle of journaling with a scriptural call for "action?"

2. According to Matthew 7:3-5, who needs to be first to deal with their rebellion and sin?

3. According to 2 Chronicles 7:13-14, who needs to be first to humble themselves, pray, and seek God's face, and turn from their wicked ways (repent)?

4. If our vertical relationship is not healthy, how can we expect our horizontal relationships to reconcile?

CHAPTER ONE

"Therefore everyone who hears these words of Mine and does them will be like a wise man who built his house on the rock."
- Jesus (Matthew 7:24)

"I call the heavens and the earth to witness about you today, that I have set before you life and death, the blessing and the curse. Therefore choose life so that you and your descendants may live, by loving Adonai your God, listening to His voice, and clinging to Him. For He is your life and the length of your days."
- Adonai in conversation with Moses: Deuteronomy 30:19-20a

www.TheBibleProject.com
- Search Blessing and Cursing

"Sin had brought a curse upon all the nations of the earth. God called Abraham to follow him because he wanted to bless all the nations of the earth through Abraham's descendants. It didn't take long to realize that God's desire to bless human beings begins in the very first chapter of Genesis and culminates in the last chapter of the last book with a grand vision of healing for all nations.

The implication was obvious: The Bible was claiming that I should read it because it was written to bless my nation and me. The revelation that God wanted to bless my nation of India amazed me." - Vishal Mangalwadi, The Book That Made Your World

In Deuteronomy 30:19-20 we find these words, given by God and recorded by Moses:

*I call the heavens and the earth to witness about you today, that I have set before you life and death, the blessing and the curse. Therefore **choose life** so that you and your descendants may live, by loving ADONAI your God, listening*

19

to His voice, and clinging to Him. For He is your life and the length of your days, that you may dwell on the land that ADONAI swore to your fathers—to Abraham, to Isaac and to Jacob—to give them.

It is upon this Scripture that I discovered the title of the Choose Life Journal system. Choosing life was a choice given by God to the nation of Israel. Why would they, or any of us, want anything other than life? Yet every day we are faced with the choice of choosing life or a curse.

Proverbs 18:21 says, "Death and life are in the control of the tongue." Yet, how many of us explode with language that would peel the paint off a wall? This past summer I was out for my daily walk, and because of the nice weather someone's front door was open. A heated conversation was going on inside and every other word was four letters long. Yes, I have heard it before, but we are not cautious about the damage we do. That kind of language is character assassination of the highest order.

Fathers, uncles and brothers! When we exhibit this toxic behavior, we are also modeling a lifestyle which our children, nieces and nephews walk out the door and repeat. If you don't believe me, here is another example from my school bus driving days. I was driving a small bus for elementary special needs children and only two boys were on board. At this age, they all have backpacks and assigned seats. The routine provides stability. The two boys come onboard and go to their assigned seats and buckle their seat belts and we are underway. I just got on the main thoroughfare and the little boy in the front seat goes ballistic. He is looking for his jacket and thinks he has left it back in his classroom. In no uncertain terms he begins to kick the panel in front of him, yelling and screaming for me to turn this ****bus around so he can get his jacket! Unfortunately, his teacher had stuffed his coat in the bottom of his backpack, and he could not see to the bottom where the jacket was. I quickly radioed dispatch and secured permission to reroute and take him home first! It took him some time to decompress. Fortunately, the other little boy didn't get triggered and sat back and enjoyed the ride. My point is this. He was repeating the language he heard from home. No six- or seven-year-old should be talking like an adult who is out of control.

In the book of Mark (Chapter 5), we see, exhibited in the life of Jesus, an exchange with a demoniac, a man who lived among the tombs, who is characterized by yelling and screaming and terrorizing the community. He was gashing himself with stones. So, he was not only terrorizing others, he was terrorizing himself. When Jesus

20

approached him, it was the demons who spoke to Jesus begging Him not to "terrorize them." Can you imagine, they who were the terrorists, plead not to be terrorized. If you don't know Jesus, one of the claims He makes of Himself is found in John 10:10, *"The thief comes to steal, slaughter, and destroy. I have come that they might have life, and have it abundantly."*

Do you hear the contrast? It certainly was not Jesus who was terrorizing this man, but demons who do satan's bidding. Jesus casts out the demons, and notice the man's immediate condition, *"He was sitting there, dressed (he was previously naked) and in his **right mind**."* One of the sad realities of many of our homeless is the prevalence of mental illness. Seattle is plagued with tent cities and people living on the streets.

I applaud those like Mario Murillo who go into areas that most of us avoid. We need people who are skilled with the Word of God and deliverance ministry. This is a return to the early Ekklesia ministry in the power of the Holy Spirit.

What is interesting to me about this account is the response of the community who was also delivered from the terror of the demons. "And they began to beg Yeshua to leave their country." But notice, the delivered man "kept begging to remain with Him." The community couldn't stand the disruption to their lives, but the man who was delivered could not get enough. He wanted more!

Do we want more of Jesus? Or are we satisfied with the status quo? Do we want to see peace brought to tormented people? Or don't we care?

Jesus' response to the now peaceful, in his right mind man, "Go home to your friends and tell them how much Adonai has done for you, how He has showed you mercy."

When is the last time you testified of what Jesus has done for you? What difference would it make in the lives of your friends and loved ones if you testified of Jesus' love and grace?

Are we actively seeking and choosing life today? Or are we perpetuating the curse through our tongues, through our words?

FOR GROUP DISCUSSION

1. Do you understand the difference between choosing life and choosing death? Which examples above demonstrate life and death?

2. How do you demonstrate choosing life or death to your friends and family? Do you show life or death in your speech? In your eating? In exercise? In lifestyle choices?

3. What lifestyle change will you make today to begin Choosing Life?

4. In your small group, pray for one another regarding the lifestyle changes we agree to make today, for power and discipline in the Holy Spirit to follow through.

CHAPTER TWO

I have treasured Your Word in my heart, so that I might not sin against You. Psalm 119:5

All Scripture is inspired by God and useful for teaching, for reproof, for restoration, and for training in righteousness, so that the person belonging to God may be capable, fully equipped for every good deed. 2 Timothy 3:16

For You—magnified above all Your Name and Your Word. Psalm 138:2b

"Forgive me if I'm wrong, but I suspect that when it comes to the theme Word and Spirit, Evangelicals seem to be more interested in the Word than they are the Holy Spirit. Charismatics seem to be more interested in the Holy Spirit than they are the Word. It is my view that we must love both equally, pursue both equally, and emphasize both equally. R.T. Kendall

A person who is experienced in God's Word is one who is well trained and skillful in His Word. If a man wants to study the Bible and understand God's Word, he must be experienced in his practice.

It is a fact that a man's character and habit are often revealed through his reading of the Bible. If a man is not disciplined by God in his character and habits, he will fall into total error, and his reading of the Bible will be spiritually fruitless."[1]

I have thought for years that perhaps the Bible is too available, too accessible. While it is the number one all-time, best-selling, book ever written, it is extremely undervalued. Many people have a copy of the Bible, but rarely open it. Would we value and treasure it more if, as a book, it was required of us to dig for it, like mining for precious gems?

---

1   Watchman Nee, *How to Study the Bible* @1993

If we had to dig tunnels and excavate tons of dirt before we could find even one precious gemstone, would we do it? Would we pay the price if we had to use a shovel rather than an excavator? Would we do it alone rather than as a group, or team, or crew?

In 2010 a reality show named Gold Rush launched on the Discovery Channel. The show followed the lives of various teams of men who went to Alaska in search of gold. They experienced the heartbreak and failure of equipment break down and the difficulty of life apart from their families, mixed with levels of success in finding the precious ore.

There was no guarantee of finding the illusive valuable ore. However, while bank accounts were exhausted in securing equipment and ferrying it north to claim sites, they experienced little of what the gold miners faced who risked their lives in the gold rush fever which struck the Alaskan Klondike in 1896. Word of finding gold had reached the United States, and people streamed to Alaska in hopes of striking it rich; few did find riches.

Most had not a clue what they were facing, and many lost their lives enroute. The harsh elements of Alaskan weather claimed many lives. Here is a brief synopsis provided by Wikipedia.

"The Klondike Gold Rush was a migration by an estimated 100,000 prospectors to the Klondike region of Yukon, in north-western Canada, between 1896 and 1899. Gold was discovered there by local miners on August 16, 1896; when news reached Seattle and San Francisco the following year, it triggered a stampede of prospectors. Some became wealthy, but the majority went in vain. It has been immortalized in films, literature, and photographs."

If you have never watched a documentary on the Alaska Gold Rush, I would recommend the PBS documentary The Klondike Gold Rush | PBS or the options posted on YouTube by the History Channel or the BBC. The hardship was unimaginable and not for the faint of heart.

For many of the early prospectors it was just them and their mule. They lived lives of solitude while chasing a dream.

Somehow, we must embrace an elevated valuation of Scripture. Is the Word of God that important? It used to be that the covers of Bibles were stamped "Holy Bible." Do we understand that the Bible is holy, inspired, instructional, living, and God-breathed? Are you aware that the term God-breathed or God-inspired in the Greek is *theopneustos*? We find this concept of God breathing life into three differing events: man (Genesis 2:7), the new community of faith (Acts 2:2), and the Bible (2 Timothy 3:16).

How are these three accounts in Scripture conveying the concept of being God-breathed?

In the Genesis account we are told that God gave man the breath of life. He breathed into man, life-giving breath. Life originated in God.

In the new community found in Acts 2:2, the word for a "mighty rushing wind" is translated, "a breath violent," also initiated by God the Holy Spirit.

Then in 2 Timothy 3:16, the word "inspiration" is the Greek term *theopneustos*, or God-breathed.

Doesn't it make sense that if Jesus is alive, and He is, by convincing proof (1 Corinthians 15:3-8), that His Word and His people should be alive too? This concept is so palpable, that we should see the Bible pulsating, sitting on our desk. We should feel it pulsating when we hold and read the Scriptures. They should come alive because they are alive.

I feel right now, like I perceive S.M. Lockridge felt in his famous dissertation *That's My King* where he is trying to convey who God is to an assembling of people, "I wish I could explain Him to you." The Bible is God's Holy Word, and we are meant to heed it, obey it, listen to it, be instructed by it, walk according to it, honor it, hide it in our hearts, memorize it, ponder it, and we are commanded not to "add or take away" from this book or we will suffer horrendous consequences (Revelation 22:18-19).

Amazing benefits accompany the study of the Bible, God's Holy Word. Here is what Paul tells a young Timothy about God's Word. It is,

"useful for teaching, for reproof, for restoration, and for training in righteousness, so that the person belonging to God may be capable, fully equipped for every good deed" (2 Timothy 3:16).

What Paul is telling Timothy is that it is impossible apart from the study of God's Word to obtain righteousness. Like Paul, I will not say that I have attained righteousness but the result of my study of the Word, combined with the work of the Holy Spirit, I have experienced a transformation which Paul speaks of in Romans 12:2, "*Do not be conformed to this world but be transformed by the renewing of your mind.*" Something we all desperately need as followers of Yeshua.

Here is another amazing benefit of the study of the Bible. The Bible is a powerful book and is able (my paraphrase) to do spiritual surgery on us. Most of us know the concept of physical surgery. I have experienced two back surgeries over the course of my life, one in 1995 and then again in 2019. When all other non-surgical modality options failed to relieve the sciatic symptoms, surgery was needed.

Here is what the writer of Hebrews says,

For the Word of God is living and active and sharper than any two-edged sword—piercing right through to a separation of soul and spirit, joints and marrow, and able to judge the thoughts and intentions of the heart (Hebrews 4:12).

In the midst of severe pain, mixed with the intense desire for the relief of that pain, I have opted for surgery at the hands of a skilled physician. I find it interesting that we will run to a medical doctor, but we will resist the Creator's healing.

One of my favorite Psalms (103) begins like this,

Bless the Lord, O my soul and all that is within me, bless His holy name. Bless the Lord, O my soul and forget not all His benefits. He forgives our iniquity. He heals all your diseases...

The word "all" is significant. Why shouldn't He heal all diseases? After all, He is the Creator and knows our bodies intimately. Who is more capable of healing us than God? No one!

I have not had the experience of traveling to China, but I have heard testimony of missionaries, that because of the outlawing of Bibles and the scarcity of Bibles, the Chinese people prize the Word of God so much that they many times tear pages or books out of the printed Bible and parcel it out with one another. They take it and memorize it and then pass it along to another. The benefit of memorizing the Bible is this, it cannot be taken away from you!

I have included the memories of a good friend, Joe Monroe, regarding his experiences traveling to China with a group of college friends. You can find the accounting of his trip to China as an addendum in this book.

My hope in writing this chapter is to create a value for the Word of God which compels you to seek to know God through the pages of the letters which were inspired by the Spirit for our benefit years ago. The Bible is our instruction manual.

I know that many of you, like myself, have tried to assemble an item without referencing the accompanying instructions, only to sort through the recycle bin to find them. Many of us have tried to live our lives without reading the instructions given to us by God. How did that work for you?

Not accessing the instructional manual of the Word of God did not work well for me. When I discovered a system of inductive Bible study in 2005, my life began to transform. I contend that when we get into the Word, the Word gets into us and transforms us, just as those who were healed by Jesus while He was on the earth. One touch from Him and their lives were changed forever.

I encourage you to get into the greatest instructional manual every written, by the One who created us. In 1 Corinthians 10:11, the apostle Paul says this, "Now these things happened to them as an example, and it was written down as a warning to us—on whom the ends of the ages have come." If we do not read the Bible, we cannot heed the warnings because we are not aware. We remain ignorant, but there is no need for ignorance of the Word if we can read. The warnings are there in plain sight for everyone.

I want to end with the words of a hymn I was taught as a child. The title is "Holy Bible, Book Divine," music written by William B. Bradbury and text by John Burton.

Holy Bible, Book Divine

Holy Bible, book divine,
Precious treasure thou art mine;
Mine to tell me whence I came;
Mine to teach me what I am.

Mine to chide me when I rove;
Mine to show a Savior's love;
Mine thou art to guide and guard,
Mine to punish or reward.

Mine to comfort in distress,
Suff'ring in this wilderness;
Mine to show by living faith,
Man can triumph over death.

Mine to tell of joys to come
And the rebel sinners doom;
O thou Holy Book divine,
Precious treasure, thou are mine.

FOR GROUP DISCUSSION

1. Do you value the Word of God? How do you show God that you value His Word?

2. How do you show others how you value God's Word?

3. How do you show your family that you value God's Word?

4. How do you show yourself that you value God's Word?

Action: I show God I value His Word when I, _____ (fill in the blank). Knowing this, I will _____(fill in the blank).

CHAPTER THREE

ATHLETICS, MUSICIANSHIP, AND MY DENTIST!

*Don't you know that in a stadium the runners all run, but one
receives the prize? Run in such a way that you may win!
1 Corinthians 9:24*

*Therefore, since we have such a great cloud of witnesses
surrounding us, let us also get rid of every weight and entangling
sin. Let us run with endurance the race set before us, focusing on
Yeshua, the initiator and perfecter of faith. Hebrews 12:1-2a*

"Pride + Poise = Victory"
- Dennis Johnson Kent-Meridian HS Football Coach

"He who can, does. He who can't, teaches."
- George Bernard Shaw

How often do I need to floss?
Every day!
How many of my teeth do I need to floss?
Only the ones you want to keep!
- My dentist, anonymous!

I launched my football career in my 9th grade year of junior high school. Most kids today experience their 9th grade in high school, but in my day, it was a part of junior high.

I first played organized sports as I entered junior high, beginning with basketball, and then I added track, and finally football. By any standard, I was late in starting sports, and much behind the eight ball. The boys who had played starting in 7th grade already knew the system of blocking, tackling, and the plays. So, I played very little my first year.

I was not dissuaded by the fact that I didn't play. In fact, it made me more determined. I had experienced the same type of coaching in 8th grade basketball. A new coach had been hired straight out of college and he ran his program like a college program. It nearly broke me as I made every practice but never played one minute of game time. I cried many times after games on the ride home. My mother tried to convince me to quit, but for me that was not an option.

Junior high is tough, and boys that age do a lot of growing up emotionally and physically, or they are weeded out. I remember two brothers who were all-stars in junior high because they developed earlier than the rest of us. But by high school, the rest of the boys had matured and caught and surpassed them. Neither of the bothers played as starters in high school. The transition was dynamic.

By my sophomore year, I was a starter on my class team. By my Junior year I lettered in Varsity football, setting up a senior year where we were undefeated in league placing us in a championship game at Seattle's Memorial Stadium, on the Space Needle's shadow, against the Metro Champ Ingraham Rams.

My team as a class was undefeated for three years and this was the pinnacle of our achievement. A bunch of boys from Kent, which at the time was considered a farming community, were going to the big city to play their best. The game was aired on radio and got a lot of press coverage. A convoy of school buses brought our fans and the marching band.

It was like an away game for us because the Rams were playing in their home stadium. Memorial Stadium was carpeted with AstroTurf, which was new to us. All the stadium fields in our league were grass turf fields. Because AstroTurf was new to us, none of our players had the proper shoes. So, the University of Washington loaned us shoes for that game. We got out of school for one day to go to the UW athletic department and were fitted with shoes. We were even allowed to familiarize ourselves with the shoes on AstroTurf at Husky Stadium. Pretty heady stuff.

The game was played on Thanksgiving Day, November of 1970. We felt extremely confident and prepared. At game time the temperature was 32 degrees and the weather forecast predicted snow. It was cold, and to compound the frigid temperatures, AstroTurf holds water. Every tackle ended in a splash. From the first plays our uniforms were soaked.

It was a tough day for the Royals. We won the coin toss and set ourselves up for a kickoff return that never happened. The Rams had obviously scouted us well and saw a tendency that caused them to onside kick the opening play. I have never seen an onside kick on the opening play in all my years of watching college or professional football. And yes, they recovered the ball. They only went three plays and out, but it set a tone for the rest of the game which they won 22-0. It was a miserable way to end my high school football career.

Why did I share this story with you? Certainly not to boast. Very few players from that team went on to play college football. Only one went on to play Division 1 football and later was drafted and played in the NFL.

I told you my story so I could tell you what sports, music and brushing your teeth have in common. They have one word in common, "discipline." To be good at anything takes discipline. Athletes practice, and many today work out the entire year, maintain a strict diet and get proper sleep. Musicians practice for hours, create muscle memory doing scales, take care of their instrument and body.

Many hours are spent in anonymity, alone, being a nobody in the sports world or music world, long before being recognized.

Even our dental habits require the daily discipline of flossing and brushing.

Through my years of personal, daily Bible study, I discovered Galatians 5:22, which says,

> But the fruit of the Ruach is love, joy, peace, patience, kindness, goodness, faithfulness, gentleness, and self-control.

Did you catch the last characteristic of the Spirit's fruit? In some translations, self-control is called discipline. I have witnessed a major lack of self-control or self-discipline among Christians. In fact, I am guilty of not exercising self-control until I saw it listed in the fruit of the Ruach.

By the time you read this, it will have been three years since I went on a food control plan and lost 33 pounds and have kept most of it off. But I did not accomplish that goal (it was intentional), until I knew my "why" and then employed a plan.

My why was health. I wanted to avoid the health concerns which run in my family. I wanted to have a healthier lifestyle. I wanted to be mobile and stay mobile. I knew I was a "carboholic," and I could choose to change my diet or suffer later. I also greatly reduced my sugar intake. The combination of those changes with reduced caloric intake and walking daily, have made the difference.

As Christians, where else do we see the lack of self-control or discipline? I believe our lifestyle should demonstrate self-control as it is an ability given to us by the Holy Spirit. Do we possess the capability or not? Can we, with the Holy Spirit's help, control our tongue, our weight, our consumption of food, our gaming habit, our sports addiction, cigarettes, alcohol, social media, television, movies, or you name it? Can we claim to have the Holy Spirit and not exercise self-control?

Self-control is a monitoring factor, a major difference between someone who is Spirit-filled and living for Jesus and someone who is rebellious and living for self.

It takes "discipline" to schedule time with God. So many things can get in the way. I hope you will consider that even the discipline of flossing your teeth is a demonstration of self-control unto God. Teeth are a part of the temple in which the Ruach dwells. Let's take care of our temple well.

FOR GROUP DISCUSSION

1. Is the issue of self-control or discipline lacking in your life? If so, please share one safe area of your struggle to discipline yourself.

2. Are there other fruits found in Galatians 5:22 with which you would like the Holy Spirit's help?

3. In which area of intentional change do you want to take action today?

CHAPTER FOUR

"That's My King.... Yeah! I wish I could describe Him to you!"
S.M. Lockridge

Taste and see how good Adonai is. Blessed is the one
who takes refuge in Him. Psalm 34:9 TLV

I have noticed a growing trend in and among Christian circles. A popular trend towards devotional time rather than an intimate, personal time of study in the Word. The tradeoff is experience.

I have always loved the personal discipline that music and sports have brought to my life. My first love as a young boy was baseball. I loved playing so much that personal injury could not stop me.

I was born in the plains of Kansas to two Nebraska-born Cornhuskers. My early childhood summer days were spent barefoot playing outdoors. The neighborhood kids would come to our backyard to play. Never was there a lack of activity. Mostly games of kick the can or keep away. Plenty of running and chasing.

I recall one day stepping on a nail which penetrated deeply into my heel. I was moaning and groaning, hobbling around, and complaining about how much it hurt. I didn't know my mother was a psychologist, but she matter-of-factly said, "I guess you won't be able to play in the baseball game tonight."

I believe in miracles and healing, but the power of that statement transitioned me into a miracle healing right now! "I'm ok!" There was nothing short of being hospitalized that was going to keep me from playing baseball that night. It truly was a miraculous healing of my heel.

My healing didn't require a squirt of Bactine, a Band-Aid, or a kiss. Just the magic words, "I guess you can't play tonight!" My mom skipped all the usual protocol and spoke healing into being. She knew how much I wanted to play.

I will give new moms another insight. Moms know when their

children are sick or not and they know when their kids are getting well. One of my mother's favorite sayings was, "I know you are sick when you are too sick to fight with your brother. I know you are getting well when you begin to fight." When I was truly sick, I didn't care about what he was doing. I was caught up in how I felt - miserable. But, when I began to feel good, I cared about what my brother was doing.

So, I made the game that night, no problem. I didn't tell the coach because I wanted to play. I played through the pain; I overcame.

What does personal injury have to do with studying the Bible? Reading a devotional is like living the Christian life through the thoughts, feelings, and personal experiences of someone else. It is vicarious living at the best.

I have loved and enjoyed sports all my life. I loved watching my children as they played sports. My son loved baseball and my daughters both played club and school volleyball. One of my daughters had the privilege of playing on a high school team which participated in two State volleyball tournaments. She thrived and excelled as a team captain and setter for the Varsity team. This team was so fun to watch.

This experience has already been over 20 years ago. Hard to imagine, but I still remember that it was the girls who played club during the high school team off-season, whose teams excelled in league, district, and state championships. It was the girls who paid the price, both financially and physically, to be the best.

I will never forget a particular Saturday at a club tournament. My daughter and I were sitting near each other during a game break and she and some friends were talking about church attendance. Several differing faiths were represented. I am not sure of all the girls' faiths, but I knew one of the other team captains, an all-league player whose family were devout Mormon members. My daughter commented that she knew what she believed and did not need to attend church. The danger of this attitude is that we assume the same posture about studying and reading the Bible.

At an appropriate moment, I piggybacked on the conversation and asked my daughter, "If you dressed in your uniform and sat in the stands at games or tournaments, what would you be called? What do you call someone in uniform and playing in the game?" She didn't respond.

My concern is that we can deceive ourselves into thinking we have a personal relationship with God when we are living a vicarious relationship with God through someone else. We could be relying

on our pastor. How many times have I heard someone say, "I attend
_____ _____ Church and I listen to ___ ____ pastor.

ARE YOU VICARIOUSLY LIVING OUT YOUR CHRISTIAN FAITH?

Let's not be guilty of living our lives before God through the teachings, sayings, devotionals, sermon notes, of anyone else, but may we directly, personally interact with God through the Holy Spirit. Anything less is not a personal relationship. Allow the Holy Spirit to be your mentor, your teacher, the One who leads you into all truth.

I'll give you another example for those of us who are married or have been married. Would you say you had a personal relationship with your spouse if every day, rather than meeting with your spouse or talking with your spouse, you read a devotional written by someone else who told you about your spouse from their perspective? Would you or your spouse consider that you had a personal relationship with each other?

THERE IS MARRIAGE IN HEAVEN!

Most of us are going to be shocked by my next statement because we have been told that there is no marriage in heaven. Some of you are relieved others are disappointed but here is what my Bible says,

> *Then I heard something like the voice of a great multitude—*
> *like the roar of rushing waters or like the rumbling of*
> *powerful thunder—saying,*
>
> > *"Halleluyah!*
> > *For Adonai Elohei-Tzva'ot reigns!*
> > *Let us rejoice and be glad*
> > *And give the glory to Him!*
> > *For the wedding of the Lamb has come,*
> > *And His bride has made herself ready,*
> > *She was given fine linen to wear,*
> > *bright and clean*
> > *For the fine linen is*
> > *The righteous deeds of the kedoshim*
> > *Revelation 19:6-8.*

There is marriage in heaven and only one wedding. We will be married, just not to each other. Jesus is the Bridegroom, we are the bride. Are you preparing and getting to know your Husband while on earth? You can only accomplish this through a daily, personal time with God, led by the Holy Spirit. This requires one-on-one, personal interaction with God. This is the Berean lifestyle Paul records in Acts 17:10-12, "because they received the message with good will, searching the Scriptures each day to see whether these things were true."

This was the lifestyle and character of the Berean people. They were not in the business of refuting the apostles, but rather by the study of the Word they were affirming that what was being told them was true! We must study for the same purpose, so that we will know the truth of the Word.

If a person, male or female, pastor/theologian or someone untrained in Scripture, teaches or preaches the Word and misquotes or misinterprets the passage, how can you know whether what they are saying is accurate, unless you search the Word for yourself? The simple answer is you cannot know. This is how the world can hijack religion and shame us regarding who God is.

It is horrifying to me how the community of faith can be taken hostage by a world who doesn't know God or His Word yet purports to know Scripture as they quote it all the time. Know this, their father is the master accuser and he quoted Scripture in attempting to deceive Yeshua in the desert. Why should we expect any different response from an accusing spirit? The only way we can defend ourselves is by knowing the Scriptures and discerning the spirits of accusation (1 John 4:1). Remember, *"the sword of the Spirit, which is the Word of God"* (Ephesians 6:17b). Keep the sword of the Spirit at the ready position. It is your defense and offense!

FOR GROUP DISCUSSION

1. Have you ever read and studied the entire Bible from Genesis through Revelation?

2. What are the advantages of studying the entire Bible? What are the disadvantages of not studying the entire Bible?

3. How much of the Bible have you read and studied? Is it possible to have a solid understanding of who God is if you have only studied a portion of the Bible?

4. Why is it important to study the entire Bible? Why is it important to study the Bible every day?

CHAPTER FIVE

Do not store up for yourselves treasures on earth,
where moth and rust destroy and where
thieves break in and steal (Matthew 6:19).

As a Kingdom of priests, we know that it is our
responsibility to rule the world for God by our prayers.
- Derek Prince, Secrets of a Prayer Warrior

Prayer is essentially a partnership of the redeemed
child of God working hand in hand with God
toward the realization of His redemptive purposes on earth.
- Dutch Sheets, *Intercessory Prayer: How God Can Use Your
Prayers to Move Heaven and Earth*

I selected the word "PRA(A)YER" for the Choose Life acronym for several critical reasons, one being that it is the only request made from The Twelve: that Jesus teach them to pray. What the Disciples heard and witnessed of Jesus was a life devoted to conversation with His Father.

The gospel writers record numerous accounts of Jesus finding a place of solitude and praying to His Father. We see in the last days of His journey to the cross, late night and early morning travailing prayer with the Father.

Prayer was so critical to Jesus, and it is so critical to us if we are going to follow His example. If He modeled a lifestyle of prayer to the apostles, was He not also modeling this lifestyle for us? If prayer recharged His batteries, will it not also recharge our spirit? If prayer is a crucial action in Jesus' relationship with His Father, is it not also vital to our relationship with Jesus and God?

John records these words spoken by Jesus,

> [19] *Therefore Yeshua answered them, "Amen, amen I tell you, the Son cannot do anything by Himself. He can do only what He sees the Father doing. Whatever the Father does, the Son does likewise.* [20] *For the Father loves the Son and shows Him*

everything He does. He will show Him even greater works than these, so that you will be amazed. [21] For just as the Father raises the dead and gives them life, so also the Son gives life to whomever He wants (John 5:19-21).

If Jesus declares that miracles, healings and casting out demons is only accomplishable by *prayer and fasting* (Mark 9:28-29), can we do any less?

Do you see that from the reading and studying of Scripture, Jesus models a lifestyle which the Holy Spirit builds within us? The Holy Spirit calls it *transformation* and *conformation* to Jesus. Under the inspiration of the Holy Spirit, Paul best captures this process in Romans 12:1-2:

I urge you therefore, brothers and sisters, by the mercies of God, to present your bodies as a living sacrifice—holy, acceptable to God—which is your spiritual service. [2] Do not be conformed to this world but be transformed by the renewing of your mind, so that you may discern what is the will of God—what is good and acceptable and perfect.

We all need to be transformed and conformed to Christ's image. For most of us, life has beaten us up and squeezed us into the world's image. Most of us have no clue how worldly we have become in our thought processes, which have shaped our hearts into coldness and hardness. We have not become conformed to Christ's image if we have not engaged with the Holy Spirit in combination with the Word, in the process of transformation. We love to quote 2 Corinthians 5:17, "*[17] Therefore if anyone is in Messiah, he is a new creation. The old things have passed away; behold, all things have become new.*" But even though we are a new creation in Christ (according to Paul's second letter to the Corinthians), if we have not put in the time, we are still operating in the flesh and not the Spirit.

This is a lifetime process my friends. Let us not think that we have arrived just because we have been born again. We have only just begun this new life with Jesus. We have much to learn and much transformation to process. Be patient with yourself, but not complacent. He is patient with us because He understands. But let's not use God's patience and understanding for license to sin.

So, allow me to describe and define what each letter of the PRAAYER acronym stands for:

P*: Stands for Prayer and reminds us to go to prayer as the first element of studying the Scriptures. Ask for the Holy Spirit's help in understanding what you are going to read from the

Word of God. Ask for new insight and fresh awareness of biblical principles for living a Christ-like lifestyle. By appealing for the Holy Spirit's help in gleaning understanding, you are admitting your need for help in the process. Know that the Holy Spirit's role is to bring you into all truth. Jesus promises us that the Holy Spirit will fulfill and accomplish this in the lives of Jesus' followers. There is only "one" Holy Spirit, and He is tasked with several things including leading us into all truth.

> [13] But when the Spirit of truth comes, He will guide you into all the truth. He will not speak on His own; but whatever He hears, He will tell you. And He will declare to you the things that are to come. [14] He will glorify Me, because He will take from what is Mine and declare it to you. [15]Everything that the Father has is Mine. For this reason I said the Ruach will take from what is Mine and declare it to you (John 16:13-15).

I encourage you to solicit the help of the Holy Spirit from the onset of your time with God. Asking the Holy Spirit to engage with you in understanding the Word launches your day with a supernatural ignition!

R: Reading the Bible with a systematic, daily approach gives continuity to your study.

Our reading plan has been designed in such a way to provide flexibility.

- If you want to take a slower, deeper approach to your study, then do one tier every year.
- If you want to read the entire Bible from Genesis to Revelation in a single year, then read the daily schedule for each tier.
- The first three tiers take you through the New and Old Testaments.
- Tier 4 is a Wisdom Literature focus utilizing the Psalms, Proverbs and Ecclesiastes.

My suggestion is to do Tier 4 in combination with any other tier, and if you are new to the Scriptures, begin with the New Testament as this reading plan begins with John. The chapter-by-chapter approach will provide you with an overview of every book in the Bible.

We promote an inductive approach to Bible Study. To understand how to do an inductive approach, please read Chapter 7 on inductive Bible Study. If you are new to this method of Bible study, you may also refer to the back of this book for a launching point in the book of John.

A*:* Attention. Which specific verses jump off the page and give you an "Oh wow!" moment? Which verses (please limit to a couple verses), grab your attention and give you fresh directive for a biblical lifestyle? Some days, I may have a couple options in journaling, so when that happens, I often lift up a quick prayer asking the Holy Spirit which attention grabber is most important. I have found that from year to year I select different verses, concepts, and principles to write about.

A word to those who are new to inductive Bible study and those who are newborn in Christ. Write at your level. It's okay to keep your journal entries simple.

The illustration I will give you is comparable in the spiritual, to the physical. We would not expect children to be writing at a high school level at five years of age. You will find, that with every passing year, discoveries continue and awareness increases. There is a process of maturing spiritually just as we age physically. Engage in the process with the Holy Spirit for the long term.

I heard a pastor years ago phrase our journey with the Holy Spirit this way: "We are saved, we are being saved, and will ultimately, one day be saved." Commit yourself to Jesus, for the long-haul, which is called "eternity."

A*:* Action is the secret sauce! Action is the application of the Word! James (Jacob), says it this way:

²² But be doers of the Word, and not hearers only, deluding yourselves. ²³ For if anyone is a hearer of the Word and not a doer, he is like a man who looks at his natural face in a mirror— ²⁴ for once he looks at himself and goes away, he immediately forgets what sort of person he was. ²⁵ But the one who looks intently into the perfect Torah, the Torah that gives freedom, and continues in it, not becoming a hearer who forgets but a doer who acts—he shall be blessed in what he does (James 1:22-25).

Why do I call "action" the secret sauce? Because action is *that* crucial to our lifestyle in Jesus.

Action is what created a non-profit organization called The Widows Project which I founded in 2015 and is now in France, Mexico, and several countries neighboring Mexico.

Action has created the Choose Life Journal program.

Action is what compelled me to author the books I have written.

Without writing hundreds of action statements, I would never have accomplished what I have.

I have told numerous people, that if you write enough action statements, you will eventually *do* something because the Holy Spirit is credited with the task of convicting us of sin. You see, it is sin to know what to do and then not do it (James 4:17). May we all be *doers* of the Word and not deceive ourselves. Learn how to write good action statements and you will see your life transformed. Action is transformational!

Y: Yielding to Jesus is an act of submission. There was a hymn which I grew up on which awesomely supports the concept of yielding to Jesus. The title is:

I Surrender All.[2]

All to Jesus I surrender, All to Him I freely give;
I will ever love and trust Him, In His presence daily live.

All to Jesus I surrender, Humbly at His feet I bow,
Worldly pleasures all forsake, Take me Jesus, take me now.

All to Jesus I surrender, Make me, Savior, wholly Thine;
May Thy Holy Spirit fill me, May I know Thy pow'r divine.

All to Jesus I surrender, Lord, I give myself to Thee;
Fill me with Thy love and power, Let Thy blessing fall on me.

Refrain:
I surrender all,
I surrender all,
All to Thee, my blessed Savior,
I surrender all.

Yielding ourselves in humility is one of the hardest things for our pride. The greater our humility and submission, the greater our use. He must have human instruments which are submitted to Him.

E: Engagement with Scripture and the Holy Spirit is crucial for transformation. God wants you to engage with Him. The model prayer which Jesus gave us, and which the Emissaries (Apostles)

---

2   Public domain. Text: Judson W. VanDeVenter Music: Winfield S. Weeden

requested (teach us to pray, Luke 11:1), we see fully quoted in Matthew 6:9:

> *9 "Therefore, pray in this way:*
> *'Our Father in heaven,*
> *sanctified be Your name.*
> *There is not a father who does not desire to have his children approach him and asking of him. In fact, Jesus tells us to "ask" ...*
> *7 "Ask, and it shall be given to you. Seek, and you shall find. Knock, and it shall be opened to you. 8 For everyone who asks receives, and the one who seeks finds, and to the one who knocks it shall be opened (Matthew 7:7-8).*

God desires our engagement with Him. This is a great moment to make an appeal to you to engage with the Holy Spirit and with God. There has been, in recent years, a popularity of devotional materials available to the faith community. I have used some of them.

What I have found is this, the longer I have engaged with in a journaling process with an inductive Bible approach, the less satisfying I find the devotional process. Why?

Allow me to explain it this way. Would you want to engage with your spouse in an interpersonal relationship, or would you prefer to read someone else's thoughts, feelings, emotions about relationship with your spouse?

Devotions are someone else's thoughts about the God we say we have a personal relationship with. Devotions cause us to live relationship with God vicariously through their eyes.

Are we really willing to settle for less than a full interpersonal relationship with the Supreme King of the Universe? It just seems the lazy way out and less than personal. Let's not fool ourselves. Let's choose a complete and fully engaged personal relationship with God.

R*: Relationship with God is really what this is all about. Right? The Apostle Paul stirs me up when I read his testimony about relationship with the living God. Listen to this:

> *7 But whatever things were gain to me, these I have considered as loss for the sake of the Messiah. 8 More than that, I consider all things to be loss in comparison to the surpassing value of the knowledge of Messiah Yeshua my Lord. Because of Him I have suffered the loss of all things; and I consider them garbage in order that I might gain Messiah*

⁹ and be found in Him not having my righteousness derived from Torah, but one that is through trusting in Messiah—the righteousness from God based on trust. ¹⁰ My aim is to know Him and the power of His resurrection and the sharing of His sufferings, becoming like Him in His death— ¹¹ if somehow I might arrive at the resurrection from among the dead. Philippians 3:7-11

Can't you just hear the passion of Paul's heart as he declares, "I want to know the power of Messiah's resurrection. I want to be where He is. I want to be with Him." In fact, there are times Paul is conflicted. He knows he will win if he dies and win if He stays (Philippians 1:22-26). Do you hear his heartbeat? That is why he can say, *"For to me, to live is Messiah and to die is gain"* (Philippians 1:21).

Paul's aim, his goal, is to know Messiah! This is my goal. Is this your goal too?

Knowing God does not come through living a distracted, compromising lifestyle. Knowing God comes from an intentional, disciplined, daily Berean lifestyle engaging with the Holy Spirit who does the transforming. We can be born again and never open a Bible, never engage with the Holy Spirit and remain a carnal, baby Christian, or we can have our minds, hearts and souls transformed into His image. We can become mature in Jesus.

Just one observation from my years of studying and readdressing the Scriptures. In Galatians 5:22, Paul gives us a lengthy list of the fruits of the Spirit. Just as an exercise, please list out the 9 fruit words which Paul declares: (write them here)

1.

2.

3.

4.

5.

6.

7.

8.

9.

How did you do? Can we agree that they all are important and that no one fruit is less important?

I'll bet that most of you did all right for the first five or six but the one I am concerned about is the last one, self-control.

Did you list, "self-control?" Yes, it is a fruit of the Spirit!

As I reviewed my life back several years ago, it is the one fruit which I felt I may have lacked the most. How many of us can say that we have exercised self-control in every aspect of our lives?

I'll guarantee that most of us have at least one area of excess, which we find hard to manage and control. We have some kind of addiction which manages us, and we laugh it off. Is it a coffee addiction? Or a carb addiction? Oh, I know, you thought I was going to mention the addictions the community of faith focuses on in every message.

You see, pharisees tend to pick on the sins to which they don't have an addiction. Sin is more pervasive than we admit. Sin has a bigger definition than we know. When we know the Word, it exposes us, it convicts us.

FOR GROUP DISCUSSION

1. Which letters in the acronym "PRA(A)YER" are most impactful to you?

2. Why is prayer important to lead you into your personal time with God?

3. Why is prayer important to conclude your time with God?

4. Is "Self-Discipline" an important aspect of establishing a daily Berean lifestyle? Are you prepared to make an "Action" statement committing yourself to becoming a disciple of the Word through the Choose Life Journal plan?

CHAPTER SIX

WHAT IS UNIQUE ABOUT THE CHOOSE LIFE JOURNAL PLAN

"We proclaim Him (Messiah), warning and teaching everyone in all wisdom, so that we may present every person complete in Messiah." Apostle Paul, Colossians 1:28

The Bible was not given to increase
our knowledge, but to change lives.
- *Evangelist D. L. Moody (1837-1899)*

Intimacy with God comes by making an effort and spending as much time with Him as you can. Never forget that He is a jealous God (Exodus 20:5). If you do not like this aspect of God's nature, I'm sorry, but that is simply the way He is. God wants you to love Him for being just like He is. I can make this promise to you: get to know Him by spending time with Him, and you will find yourself over-whelmed with amazement that we have a God like Him.

I can make a second promise to you: you will never be sorry you spent time with God's Word. Whether you are a minister or a cab driver, a children's pastor or a server in a restaurant, a worship leader or an accountant—I could go on and on—get to know your Bible better than any other book. The reward is incalculable."
-R. T. Kendal, Word and Spirit

I saw a post on Facebook this week which is spot on regarding discipleship and maturity in Christ. Interestingly, it was not attributed to anyone and appears to be written in a journal. I am going to title it, "Choose Your Hard."

Choose Your Hard

Marriage is hard.
Divorce is hard.
Choose your hard!

Obesity is hard.
Being fit is hard.
Choose your hard!

Being in debt is hard.
Being financially disciplined is hard.
Choose your hard!

Communication is hard.
Not communicating is hard.
Choose your hard!

Life will never be easy!
It will always be *hard*!
But we can choose our hard!

Choose Wisely!

I might add, I have taught people this system of Bible study. I have watched as they started strong and with good intention, only to allow life to get in the way and never establish daily studying with journaling as a disciplined lifestyle. It is hard to do but it has great reward. My journey has been transformational, and it will be for you too, if you persevere! I am not perfect but, I am not the same man that I was 15+ years ago.

So:

- if you want change,
- if you desire to be more like Christ,
- if you do not like the old man who is stuck in repetitive cycles of sin,
- if you are sick and tired of being sick and tired and defeated,

I suggest, no I implore you, to engage in the Choose Life Journal system. Embrace, in your heart and mind, the concept that this is a lifetime process in a lifetime journey. I have told many, "When you get into the Word, the Word gets into you!"

If you want to fall in love with God, this is the process I implore you to embrace.

Do you know the New Testament commandment? If not, please

stop and read Matthew 22:36-40.

Some Scripture I will not quote because I want you to do some digging. This is discipleship when you are required to know where to find referenced Scripture. The Lord needs literate disciples who know Scripture location.

I recommend a printed version of the Bible for study so that you can highlight, comment, and add notes. If a Scripture is extremely impactful, consider writing the date next to that passage. You are reading history, so document your history with God.

What does this passage tell you about your relationship with God? Have you already fulfilled this commandment? I hope you recognize that this commandment is not a one and done. This is a lifetime pursuit which the true disciple must apply every day.

You have a choice. I have observed many congregants who may be octogenarians biologically and are still babies in Christ. I have visited households who display a family heirloom Bible which has only collected dust. It has never been opened for diligent daily lifetime study and guidance.

How lovely it is to visit a true disciple of Jesus and see their Bible on a table and falling apart. I visited such a household recently! Oh, how I desire for you to experience a deeply intimate relationship with the Holy Spirit!

Another reason I got into the Word was that I want to see a return and manifestation of the power of the Holy Spirit. I want to see a return to the early community of faith, what Jesus declared the "Ekklesia," in our lifetime. I desire to see the outpouring of miracles which Jesus declared, and John captured in words,

> I tell you, he who puts his trust in Me, the works that I do he will do; and greater than these he will do, because I am going to the Father. And whatever you ask in My name, that I will do, so that the Father may be glorified in the Son. If you ask Me anything in My name, I will do it."

Do I believe Jesus' words? Do you believe them? If we do, what does the application of these words mean to our lives? What do they mean to my life?

So, what is unique to the Choose Life Journal plan?

I DO THE CHOOSE LIFE JOURNAL PLAN WITH YOU.

First, I am committed to doing and sharing my journal with you every day. I know of no one in the curriculum resource of discipleship who is doing Life Journaling with you daily. I am a product of the product. My life has been transformed by this process with the Holy Spirit and Scripture and I will do it the rest of my life. I have already journaled 15+ years on my own, solo. Just me and the Holy Spirit. I will continue because the process is that dynamic! I love the Word. I love Adonai. I am still striving to love Him with my whole heart.

This I know, my vertical relationship impacts my horizontal relationship.

The health of your vertical relationship will determine the health of your horizontal relationships. We must love God before we can love our neighbor.

SCRIPTURE MEMORIZATION

This a forgotten aspect in many discipleship curricula today. I wrestled with the idea of printing out a list of the top Scriptures I would recommend memorizing and I'll add a list as an addendum later. For now, I would recommend you buy a packet of 3 x 5 cards and write out a weekly Bible verse and carry it with you throughout the day. Look at the verse several times every day; at breakfast, first break, lunch, afternoon break, dinner and before bed. If you have a spouse or small children, write out an extra copy and give it to them to join you in memorizing. If you have dinner together as a family, what would it mean to discuss the passage you studied over dinner? How would your children respond? How would your spouse respond?

LIFE VERSE.

I also would suggest that over the course of our study together this year, that you discover your life verse. If you have never heard of a life verse, it is a verse of passage which has come to have dynamic meaning to you. Over the course of 15+ years of study, I have two life verses. Acts 17:28b "In Him (Jesus) I live and move and have my being," and Colossians 1:18b," that He (God) might come to have first place in everything."

Keep on the lookout and search for a passage of Scripture which speaks to you in such dynamic ways that it jumps off the page and you claim each other.

MUSIC IS A DYNAMIC FEATURE OF WORSHIP AND MY EXPRESSION OF PRAISE!

Music is another aspect of the Choose Life Journal that is highly personal for me. I have had a love for music all my life. I have participated as a vocal musician in choirs, ensembles, quartets, as a soloist, as a director, and as an audience participant. I love to have music playing in the background of my apartment or in my car as I travel. I am so glad that music plays such a vital role in our worship of God because of the joy it brings the listener. Music deepens and enriches my worship experience.

At the end of each journal entry, we include a link to a music video. I hope you enjoy the music which is selected. We attempt to choose music which inspires us, hoping it will inspire you too.

JOURNALING WITH INTENTION

Journaling serves to document your historical and spiritual journey with God. Isn't this what God did, through men who were inspired by the Holy Spirit, for us to read centuries later? I remember years ago thinking how glad I was that I didn't live during biblical times so that my warts and poor decisions were documented for everyone to read about years later.

Journaling helps us enter the biblical narrative as we document our interaction with God, and hopefully, it becomes historical in that generations who follow may read it and benefit from our mistakes.

When I discovered 1 Corinthians 10:6 & 11, I understood why God had the Bible written and documented. It was for my benefit, so that I might avoid the same downfalls of many who lived before me. There is high value in keeping a daily journal.

We have created additional resources to assist your study of the Word. On our website, *www.firstplaceministries.com* you can subscribe to receive the Choose Life Journal daily via email, access the reading schedule (under the Tools tab), and print a copy of the Choose Life Journal template. We also encourage you to download our Choose Life Journal phone app, available free from your app store. No matter where you are, you will have unlimited access to the Choose Life Journal, reading schedule, and the Tree of Life Bible version in the palm of your hand.

To help you with the journaling concept there are online options like YouVersion which I have used. I like creating a Word document every day and cataloging each entry so that I can reference back to a specific chapter in the Bible. It is an uncomplicated way to track your spiritual growth and see the progress you have made in the Lord. I hope you will journal with me in documenting your journey with the Holy Spirit.

FOR GROUP DISCUSSION

1. What is your experience with establishing a daily Berean lifestyle of reading and journaling? Was it hard? How long did it last?

2. Have you ever read the entire Bible, Genesis through Revelation?

3. What do you see in the Choose Life Journal plan which makes you feel this plan is more achievable and makes you feel, "I can do this!"?

4. Will you commit today to launching a lifestyle of daily reading and journaling with the Choose Life Journaling plan?

CHAPTER SEVEN

GUIDELINES FOR LAUNCHING A NEW LIFESTYLE JOURNALING
TIME WITH GOD

You will seek Me and find Me,
when you will search for Me with all your heart.
- Adonai (Jeremiah 29:13)

"The path toward true holiness, therefore, is a path full of both life
and death, perils and blessings. It is a path upon which you will be
challenged, empowered, provoked, and crucified. But you will not
be disappointed. If it is God you seek, it is God you will find."
- Francis Frangipane

The following suggestions come from my own personal experience
of journaling combined with daily inductive study of the Bible. I am
seeking to provide you tools, resources, and just enough structure
to assist you in developing your personal walk with the Supreme
Adonai Elohei-Tzva'ot.

These guidelines are the product of over 15 years of utilizing the
Choose Life Journaling approach with refinements and adjustments
along the way. I hope these will be helpful.

1. **SCHEDULE THE SAME TIME DAILY**

   Psalm 5:4

   Psalm 119:147

   There are several Psalms which declare the psalmists desire
   to meet God in the morning. I like the morning and I have
   established to give God the first fruits of my day. I find that
   giving God first priority starts my day off fabulously. I love
   meeting with God first thing. I am single so I have complete
   privacy and by meeting early I keep from distraction of
   schedule and contacts by silencing my phone. I encourage
   you to place your phone on silent mode as well. By meeting
   with God as my first appointment of the day, I confirm with
   Him and myself, that He has first place in my heart and life
   (Colossians 1:18b).

2. **MEET WITH GOD AT THE SAME PLACE EACH DAY.**

    Psalm 86:11-12

    I have a standing desk at which I work and that is my meeting place. If you do not live alone, you might have to be creative. I have heard mothers and fathers with children using their car as a private place. You might have a room in your house which is private, or you might have a favorite coffee shop which is designed for privacy. You may live in a state which the weather is good most of the time and allows you to use a gazebo, porch, or a park with a picnic table. Wherever you select to meet with God, choose a place which lends to privacy and consistency. It is your personal place to meet with God.

3. **GATHER YOUR ESSENTIALS**

    Throughout the Covid pandemic we heard the term "essential workers." Here are all the essential tools or resources you need to launch a daily lifestyle of journaling with the Choose Life Journal plan.

    A.   A BIBLE
    The most vital element is our instruction manual, the Bible. I suggest a printed version as opposed to an e-version. I like to highlight, date, make comments in my Bible. I was raised on a printed Bible, and it is my preference. I also have a preference in the version of Bible to use. If you do not already have a preference, I suggest the Tree of Life Version (TLV). Please refer to the addendum titled, Why I Like the Tree of Life Version.

    B.   A JOURNAL
    If you prefer to write your journal in long hand, you will need a pen and notebook or pad. I started my journaling journey using a spiral bound note pad. As years went on, I decided I wanted an easier way to catalog and reference my journals. So, I began creating a Word document and cataloging each journal with a dating system and titling them. Years later, I developed an acronym (PRAAYER) which reflected my approach to journaling and studying the Bible.

    C.   A BIBLE DICTIONARY & CONCORDANCE
    While most of my study ten and fifteen years ago was accomplished by utilizing an inductive Bible Study approach free from additional resources (save the Holy Spirit, the Bible and me), I do allow myself a Bible

dictionary and a concordance. I occasionally use and refer to a Holman Illustrated Bible Dictionary @2003 by Holman Bible Publishers and a New American Exhaustive Concordance of the Bible@ 1981 by the Lockman Foundation.

D. THE CHOOSE LIFE SCHEDULE

The daily schedule can be found on our website: *firstplaceministries.com*. We have designed it so that you oversee how aggressively you want to study the Bible. If you have the desire to accomplish a quicker, less intense study because you have never studied the entire Bible in a calendar year, then combining all four levels meets this requirement. This will give you an overview of the entire Bible from Genesis to Revelation.

If you want to take a slower approach and want to go deeper into each chapter and every book, then select the tier which is most beneficial to you. I encourage you to ask the Holy Spirit which approach He wants you to use.

Which ever level of study you choose to engage in, choose the level which is accomplishable with your schedule. I would rather you choose the slower approach and succeed at adding the Choose Life Journal plan as an everyday lifestyle, than to get overwhelmed and abandon in your progress. Regardless of your selection, if you do not do the full plan (the entire Bible in one year), I encourage you to add the Psalms and Wisdom Literature level with your choice.

E. DOWNLOAD THE CHOOSE LIFE APP

For the convenience of those who want to be able to access the Choose Life Journal on your phone, search your app store for the Choose Life app.

F. A REVERENT, SUBMITTED & EXPECTANT HEART

In two separate books of the Bible, Paul expresses nearly word for word the same declaration about Jesus,

"every knee shall bow to Me, and every tongue shall give praise to God" Romans 14:11b & Philippians 2:10-11.

Psalm 147:11

Our heart attitude as we approach God and His Word, is vital to our spiritual growth. Am I able to humble myself before God and His Holy Spirit to receive instruction, guidance, wisdom, spiritual nourishment, healing, transformation, forgiveness, mercy, grace, restoration, encouragement, nourishment, and discipline?

G. THE HOLY SPIRIT (RUACH)
John 14:16-17

John 16:8-15

The Holy Spirit is inseparable from our growth and understanding. He fulfills such a vital role to us and the world.

- He convicts the world about sin!
- He convicts the world about righteousness!
- He convicts the world about judgment!
- He guides you into all truth!
- He will declare to you the things that are to come.
- He will glorify Jesus!
- He will take from what is Jesus' and declare it to you!

This is what just this passage declares about the Holy Spirit, He is much more.

A Restrainer of Sin and Evil:
Did you know the Holy Spirit is a restrainer of sin? As if the sin and evil is not bad enough, it would be even worse, If He were not a restrainer of evil (2 Thessalonians 2:5-7).

A Firewall:
Did you know that the Holy Spirit prays and intercedes for you? According to Paul this is a vital part of the Holy Spirits ministry to you and me.

Romans 8:26-27

Most of us have quoted Romans 8:28 at some time in our lives without knowing what the previous two verses said. I hope you are now aware of the amazing ministry which the Holy Spirit provides to us.

I want to close with an illustration. Most of us have attempted to put together furniture or a children's playhouse without reading the instructions. I ask you; how did that work for you?

Most of us, Christians alike, attempt to live our lives without reading or consulting the Scriptures, the authoritative Word of God. How is that working for you?

If you are like me, you crashed and burned. It was through my failures that I turned to God and His Word, and I have experienced healing and transformation since. Life still has its difficulties and challenges, but I have a source of instruction in God's Word, and I have a constant mentor in the Holy Spirit.

Both the Word and the Spirit are constant and available to you and me. Invite the Holy Spirit every day to be your mentor, instructor, and guide.

I hope you will join me on this amazing journey to know God with the aid of the Holy Spirit, by engaging in the study of the Bible which was written for our instruction (1 Corinthians 10:11).

FOR GROUP DISCUSSION

1. Do you see the value of scheduling your daily time with God? My experience was until I scheduled a time, life got in the way. Please consider scheduling your time with God.

2. Why do I need to Journal? In a learning environment, we retain more of what we learn when it is written down. You also have something to refer to which reflects and affirms your growth in the Lord.

3. Why do I need to know the Bible to know God? The Bible is God's revelation or revealing of Himself. We cannot know God apart from His Word. Find a Scripture which gives a reason for knowing the Bible and knowing God (i.e., 1 Corinthians 10:11, 2 Timothy 3:16).

4. Why is the Holy Spirit necessary to my understanding of the Bible? Refer to John 15:5. I close every journal I write with the declaration, "Remember, Abide in Jesus, today!" For those who receive my journal, if you had not discovered the reason for the statement, I hope you understand now.

CHAPTER EIGHT

THERE IS AN AIRE IN MY HEART

Examples of music in the Scriptures:

There's a Song in the Air!
Hymn by Josiah G. Holland 1872 & Karl P. Harrington 1904

Scripture: Song of Miriam
Exodus 15:1-21

After singing the Hallel, they went out to the Mount of Olives.
The Lord's Supper, Matthew 26:30 & Mark 14:26

The first known use of the phrase *There's an Aire in My Heart* in print is in the December 1773 edition of the Monthly Review: "They (the Moravians and Methodists) have adopted the music of some of our finest songs... ...and they have given good reasons for so doing: for, as Whitefield said, 'Why should the devil have all the best tunes?'"

There was a statement in a song written by Larry Norman titled:

Why does the devil have all the good music?

I feel good every day, I don't wanna lose it.
All I wanna, all I wanna know
Is why should the devil have all the good music.
I've been filled, I feel okay,
Jesus is the rock and He rolled my blues
Jesus is the rock and He rolled my blues
Jesus is the rock and He rolled my blues away

Perception is the key, but deception is reality. The enemy of our souls is always counterfeiting and dubbing off the original. It has always been, it will always be. The devil, satan, is an illusionist. He will never make an original. He is always altering, corrupting, plagiarizing, copying, and counterfeiting the works and creation of God.

The truth is, God has made music from the beginning as all creation sings His praise. He says, *"if these keep silent, the stones will shout out!" (Luke 19:40b).* Have you noticed that every animal has a voice? Have you noticed the response of birds at the rising of the morning sun? Have you ever been near a rooster as a new morning dawns? Are you aware how sunflowers choreograph their movement to the sun?

Music moves my being.

I have been involved with some aspect of music most of my life. The earliest memories of music were hymn music. I am still fond of the theology I was given through the singing of hymn music. It was hymn music which I credit with forming a foundation of knowing God. Because Scripture is set to music, memorization is facilitated as we use a melody to capture the tune and words.

Recently, in a weekly phone call with my second cousin in Montana, we began singing some of the old hymns we were raised on. We must have spent 20-30 minutes just singing the first stanza of hymns as they came to mind. What an enjoyable exercise!

My involvement with music has spanned the spectrum of children's groups, Cantatas (church music before musicals; presentations which feature a narrator and a compilation of songs arranged around a theme, usually Easter or Christmas), youth choirs and musicals, small group ensembles, adult choirs, and community choirs. Most of these groups were based in the local church. I have participated in all these groups and led or directed most of them. Music has been an integral part of my worship experience, so it was natural for me to include music in the Choose Life Journal.

My reasoning was this, "If music moves me emotionally and spiritually, then I need to share the music which has impacted me."

So, I include classical music like Handel's Messiah, because the songs are scripturally based. The lyrics come straight from the Bible. I include a range of Christian music from hymns to Gaither, to Brooklyn Tabernacle to the Mormon Tabernacle (The Messiah), from Keith Green and Carmen to current contemporary artists.

Music is seen in the Scriptures.

- The angels heralded the birth of the Messiah (Luke 2:14).
- The Hebrew children composed a song after the victorious exodus titled The Song of Moses and Miriam with lyrics *"The horse and its rider He has thrown into the sea" (Exodus 15).*
- Centuries later we see the Hebrew nation singing and dancing Adonai's praise of David's victory, *"Saul has slain his thousands and David his ten thousands!"* (1 Samuel 18:7).
- The Psalms are replete with songs with lyrics and instructions to the director. Kings David and Jehoshaphat both are

credited with appointing singers to the temple service (1 Samuel 25 & 2 Samuel 20:21).

- Both Matthew (26:30) and Mark (14:26) record that Jesus and the apostles after having shared the last supper, *"after singing the Hallel, they went out to the Mount of Olives."*

Significantly, we see music mentioned in Revelation as the fulfillment of time comes to a crescendo. John explains the music he hears as:

> *a voice...like harpists playing on their harps. And they are singing a new song before the throne and before the four living creatures and the elders; and no one is able to learn the song except the 144,000 who had been redeemed for the earth (ch.14).*

Mention is made by John of the Song of Moses (Revelation 15) which we gave reference to in the book of Exodus:

> *"And they are singing the song of Moses the servant of God and the song of the Lamb, saying,*
>
> *Great and wonderful are Your deeds, ADONAI Elohei-Tzva'ot! Just and true are Your ways, O King of the nations!*
>
> *⁴Who shall not fear and glorify Your name, O Lord? For You alone are Holy. All the nations shall come and worship before You, for Your righteous acts have been revealed!*

Then, prior to the wedding of the Lamb (Revelation 19) he hears "something like the loud voice of a great multitude in heaven, shouting:

> *"Halleluyah! Salvation and glory and power belong to our God.*
>
> *²For His judgments are true and just. For He has judged the great prostitute who corrupted the earth with her whoring and has avenged the blood of His servants caused by her hand."*
>
> *³And a second time they shouted, "Halleluyah! The smoke from her goes up forever and ever!"*

Wouldn't we expect to see and hear music at a wedding as grand as the Wedding of the Lamb? Most of our weddings on earth feature a wedding march to highlight the grand entrance of the bride. In heaven, won't the focus be on the Bridegroom? Don't you anticipate that this wedding will be the Wedding of Weddings? That this celebration will be the grandest wedding ever celebrated?

FOR GROUP DISCUSSION

1. On a scale of 1-10 (one being least and 10 greatest), how important is music in your personal worship? Please explain why you gave your rating.

2. Who is your favorite Christian musical group or artist? Why?

3. What is your favorite song? Why?

CHAPTER NINE

THE TRANSFORMATIVE POWER OF THE BIBLE

All Scripture is inspired by God...
- Paul to a young Timothy

For the Word of God is living and active and sharper than any two-edged sword—piercing right through to a separation of soul and spirit, joints and marrow, and able to judge the thoughts and intentions of the heart. No creature is hidden from Him, but all are naked and exposed to the eyes of Him to whom we must give an account.
Hebrews 4:12-13

Do not be conformed to the world but be transformed by the renewing of your mind, so that you may discern what is the will of God—what is good and acceptable and perfect.
- Paul (Romans 12:2)

Regarding anointing...: "It should be what we want more than anything and what we aspire to more than any goal we can conceive. It cannot be something we seek some of the time; it must be something we pursue all of the time, every minute of every day." - R. T. Kendall

Our Good News did not come to you in word only, but also in power and in the Ruach ha-Kodesh and with complete certainty.
- Apostle Paul in the first letter to the Thessalonians 1:5

Can we begin by agreeing that our minds, our thought processes, are heavily influenced by the world media, entertainment, cartoons, gaming, advertising, public education, audio books, published books, debates, world news, social media, internet, movies? The list goes on.

Then there is the Bible.

Proportionally, what percentage of influence, impact, thought, and persuasion, does the Bible have on your life compared to the intake, invasion, domination, indoctrination, and attacks we receive minute by minute? Would you agree that there is a spiritual battle for our minds?

We are swimming in a virtual sea of counter opposition to the things of God. In fact, Paul says,

> For the mindset of the flesh is hostile toward God, for it does not submit itself to the law of God—for it cannot. So those who are in the flesh cannot please God.

Do we understand that after we come to Jesus and are born again, we must begin the process of being transformed by the Holy Spirit? Some might argue, and I hear this passage quoted all the time, "*Therefore if anyone is in Messiah, he is a new creation. The old things have passed away; behold, all things have become new.*"

It is a nice attempt to hide behind Scripture when you have done nothing about the fleshly Christian lifestyle you have adopted for yourself. God has called us to sanctification and righteousness.

Positionally, the statement by Paul is correct; however, if we have not laid our lives down and allowed the Holy Spirit to transform our lives, we cannot claim this verse.

We are redeemed, but we have chosen to stay as we are. We actually kind of like ourselves. The attitude is, "I am not so bad. I don't do this or that and I look better than most Christians I compare myself with."

Please allow me to challenge this attitude. We need not compare ourselves to anyone. Jesus is the plumbline! No one else has lived a sinless, perfect, human life. He accomplished sinless perfection because He was both God and man.

If we take the world narrative and Christianize it, we have been taken captive by the world and have not been transformed by the Holy Spirit through God's Word. Francis Schaeffer said it this way:

> *Tell me what the world is saying today,*
> *and I'll tell you what the church will be*
> *saying in seven years.*

The problem is that we are acquiescing to the world narrative and being formed and conformed to the world's image rather than transforming the world. We are either the salt and light (the influencer of our culture) or we are the culturalized. There is an influencer and an influencee. Which one are we?

Where are the days when, "Thus says the Lord" is heard from the pulpit? Where are the days when followers of Jesus embraced the authority of Scripture and heeded those words?

Here is a scriptural Plan for Reconciliation & Salvation for Eternity.

The Bible tells us ....

Who we are:

- Image Bearers: Made in God's image
  Genesis 1:26
- Loved by God: A personal relationship
  John 3:16-18
- Sinners: All Have Sinned
  Romans 3:22b-23
- Lost: Sin has separated us from God
  Isaiah 59:2

What we need:

- A Messiah: Messiah died for us
  Romans 5:8
- Reconciliation: We were still enemies of God
  Romans 5:10
- Salvation: Call on His name
  Romans 10:13

The Goal:

- Sanctification: Process of becoming holy
  1 John 1:9
- Righteousness: Process of becoming righteous
  1 John 3:7
- Conform to Yeshua: Conform to the image of Yeshua
  Romans 8:29
- Transformation: Renewing of my mind
  Romans 12:2
- Loving God and others
  Luke 10:27
- Forgiving others
  Matthew 6:14-15
- Becoming a doer of the Word
  James 1:22-25
- Presentation: Before God as tried and true
  2 Timothy 2:15
- Abiding Presence: I want to abide in Jesus
  John 15:4
- Eternal Presence: Hope of Resurrection
  1 Corinthians 15:19

Make no mistake about it. The veracity of Scripture falls in the balance of determining its authority. Satanically influenced people strategically work to discredit the authority of Scripture and attack the deity of Jesus and His resurrection by hijacking the biblical narrative and spinning a new narrative.

This is not a new tactic, it is age-old. Satan spun a new narrative about the consequence of disobedience in the garden when he said

to Eve,

> *"You most assuredly won't die. For God knows that when you eat of it,*
> *your eyes will be opened and you will be like God, knowing good and evil."*

Furthermore, he used the same tactics in the temptation of Yeshua when he asked:

- If You are Ben-Elohim: He knew who Yeshua is
- I'll give You all this authority: Authority was not his to give
- If You will worship before me: Worship belongs to God only
- If You are Ben-Elohim: He knew who Yeshua is and so did Yeshua

Just as Yeshua answered the devil with Scripture, we do well to answer him in Scripture. Therefore, I include a memory verse of the day on every journal. The value of having Scripture available on the forefront of your mind and the tip of your tongue is invaluable. Yeshua showed us how to neutralize our enemy by having Scripture at our command.

FOR GROUP DISCUSSION

1. As a group, divide up and assign to each member of your group the Scriptures listed in the Scriptural Plan for Reconciliation and Salvation. After everyone has looked up their assigned Scripture, ask them to read it aloud to the rest of the group.

2. Have everyone select one Scripture on the list to write out and memorize. Give them 5-7 minutes to write out and work on memorizing the Scripture they selected.

3. Pair up all members with someone to quote their Scripture from memory. The listening member should be prepared with the Scripture in hand to coach the quoting member. (Note to the instructor. If you have an odd number of members in your group. Please pair up with an unassigned member so that no one is left out).

4. Have everyone share what they felt when they were quoting their Scripture. Was the Scripture more impactful to you while you were quoting it? Did you feel a greater conviction about that Scripture?

5. Will you engage in regular memorization of Scripture with your journaling experience?

CHAPTER TEN

Deuteronomy 30:19-20
[19] I call the heavens and the earth to witness about you today,
that I have set before you life and death, the blessing and the
curse. Therefore choose life so that you and your descendants may
live, [20] by loving ADONAI your God, listening to His voice, and clinging
to Him. For He is your life and the length of your days, that you may
dwell on the land that ADONAI swore to your fathers—to Abraham,
to Isaac and to Jacob—to give them. - ADONAI

"The more you read God's Word, and the more you pay
attention to it, the more you will see Him use it in your life.
The more you read through it and find different verses in
different seasons of life, the more you'll find yourself saying,
"Oh, man! I never saw this before. It changes everything for me."
- Matt Rosenberg, Messianic Rabbi

Can we agree that the purpose of studying the Bible is not to
understand the greatest book ever written, but to know God
(Adonai)? And how can we know God apart from studying the Bible?

The apostle Paul tells us that the Scriptures were written for our
instruction (1 Corinthians 10:11). Paul also tells us in his letter to
the Philippians, "*My aim is to know Him (Yeshua) and the power of
His resurrection and the sharing of His suffering*" *(Philippians 3:10).*
It is under the inspiration of the Holy Spirit and through the pen of
writers like Paul that we come to know God and who He is.

The Bible is composed of 66 books: 39 in the Old Testament and
27 in the New Testament. For those new to the Bible, the delineation
between the Old and New is the coming of Yeshua, the Messiah.
The Old Testament is prior to Yeshua's birth and the New Testament
records His virgin birth, sinless life, death, burial, resurrection, and
ascension into heaven, followed by letters to the new community
of faith and finally, Revelation.

So, I begin with a question. Before you read any further, which
author wrote the biggest portion of the Bible? I can hear many of
you saying, I do not know the authors of the Bible. Fair enough.

This is also why we study the Bible, to be knowledgeable about the greatest book ever written.

Forty authors are credited with having written the Bible. Rather than listing them all, here are the top five according to volume of words: Moses, Ezra, Jeremiah, Luke, and Paul.

Do you have any idea who wrote the most volume based on words? It would be Moses as he wrote the first five books of the Bible and is credited with writing Psalm 90. Moses' writings total 125,139 words or more than 20% of the 611,000 total words of the Bible.[3]

I was surprised by my findings in doing a little online research. I thought I knew the Bible fairly well, but I learned something new in doing my research for this chapter. I never would have included Ezra as the author in second place since I had not credited him with having written 1st and 2nd Chronicles. My perception was that Isaiah would have made the top five because the book named for his writings is 66 chapters long, which is easy to remember since 66 is the number of books in the Bible.

Also, my perception was that Paul wrote more Bible content than Luke, as Paul wrote 13 books or letters to the various Communities of faith.

But in quantity, Luke authored the longest book in the New Testament, which is named after himself, and he wrote Acts. Together these two books equate to more than 6% of the Bible's total, while Paul's letters equate to just over 5%.

Let us circle back to Moses, a most incredible man. From birth, he was a child who the world was determined to terminate (Exodus 1:16). Within the land of Egypt, the nation of Israel was multiplying by the blessing of God. This caused great concern for the Pharoah, so he decreed that all baby boys be put to death. But the Hebrew midwives feared God more than they did the Pharoah and did not kill the newborn sons. Moses' mother took the precaution of giving up Moses to spare his life. She placed him in a basket of reeds and put him in the water. God's providence was upon the child Moses, and he was discovered by a daughter of Pharoah who rescued him from the water. Moses' name means "one that delivers."

Interestingly, the one who delivers was delivered by the One who delivers. _____

3   All statistics in this section were found at: https://overviewbible.com/author-wrote-most-bible/.

Oh, the providence of Adonai. Moses was discovered by a daughter of Pharoah. She summoned a Hebrew woman to be a handmaiden for the Hebrew child, and that woman was his mother. Moses received the best care and instruction growing up in the Pharoah's court. Unknown to the Pharoah, this child would one day return with the power of Adonai to deliver the Hebrew nation from the oppressive slavery His people were enduring.

I believe so much in the providence of God as I witnessed it in the move of my family from Kansas, where I was born, to Washington State where God provided for the needs of my family. My parents lost everything, a home and employment, and journeyed to Washington State, where God reestablished our family.

Moses is considered by many to be the most important prophet of the Hebrew nation. He was chosen by God to confront Pharoah and request the release of God's people, His covenant nation, from the Egyptians. It was through Moses that God chose to show his dominance over the gods the Egyptians worshipped, which culminated in the final act of God in securing the release of the Hebrew nation, the institution of Passover, and the Death Angel.

It is interesting that I am writing this account just a few weeks prior to Passover. I plan to attend a Seder Celebration this Passover. If you are not familiar with the Jewish Seder, here is a URL to a Messianic description of the observance meal: *https://youtu.be/ CfUhqDtxK6s*.

Much can be told about all the miracles which were manifested through Moses and his staff (which turned into a snake and ate the snakes of the Egyptian magicians). Frogs, gnats, flies, and locusts appeared, the Nile turned to blood, livestock died, boils broke out on the Egyptian people and their animals, hail and fire struck down the Egyptian people and their animals.

I have heard scientific experts try to explain the plagues which the Egyptian people endured as natural phenomena. However, they are unable to explain how the various plagues and severe weather touched only the Egyptians. Each of the ten plagues took a divine bypass of the Hebrew children. It was precision; divine guidance warfare at its finest.

Additionally, each of the plagues were targeted towards one of the Egyptian gods to prove the Egyptian gods as false and demonstrate God's dominion. In this way, Adonai strategically annihilated each of the false gods the Egyptians worshipped.

We could talk about the exodus of the Hebrew nation from Egypt or fleeing from slavery. The deliverance of Moses and the Hebrew nation through the parted waters of the Red Sea, and the unfolding waters which killed Pharoah's army, never to be seen again.

We could talk about the wandering years spent in the wilderness, the instructions given by God for the design and building of the Tent of Meeting, the Ark of the Covenant and all its accoutrements, the instructions for the handling of each item, and the assignment of a tribe's care of the holy items.

We could talk about Moses' travels up and down Mount Sinai and the receiving of the Torah (the Law, or what we call the Ten Commandments, Exodus 20).

We could also talk about the size of the task in moving an entire nation of people into the wilderness. Moses tells us that there were 600,000 men (Exodus 12:37), plus women and children. Even by modest estimates if each man had a wife and two children, this would equate to 2.4 million. Some estimate as high as 5-6 million Hebrew people were fleeing Egypt. Only a supernatural explanation could satisfy the level of provision needed in water and food, whether manna or quail (Exodus 16).

Just an interesting sidenote, Exodus 12:41 makes mention *that all the armies of Adonai went out from the land of Egypt.*

Was Moses referring to a heavenly host which escorted the Hebrew nation out Egypt? We know that the presence of Adonai was as a cloud by day and a pillar of fire at night. This, my friends, is supernatural protection from the sun by day and a heating source in a cold wilderness at night. They had divine protection of the Highest order! And it never left them (Exodus 13:21-22).

Moses was, no doubt, task with establishing the foundation of the worship of Adonai. To him, Adonai imparted the Torah (Exodus 20), which he was tasked with establishing in the hearts and minds of the Hebrew tribes and people. Each son of Jacob (Israel), twelve in total, was the father of a tribe, and all the tribes composed a nation (Israel). The sons in order were, Rueben, Simeon, Levi, Judah, Dan, Naphtali, Gad, Asher, Issachar, Zebulun, Joseph, and Benjamin (Genesis 35:23-26).

I share all this background information with you because Exodus 15:22-27 holds an important conversation between Adonai and Moses. Adonai instructs Moses to:

diligently listen to the voice of Adonai your God, do what is right in His eyes, pay attention to His mitzvot, and keep all His decrees, I will put none of the diseases on you which I have put on the Egyptians. For I am Adonai who heals you.

Moses was being instructed by Adonai, to tell the Hebrew nation to listen to Him, heed His Laws and obey them. If they will do this, obey His Laws, He promises them that He will not afflict them with the same diseases with which He afflicted the Egyptians. In fact, *I am the One who heals you.*

I am among those who believe that the promises of God are extended to New Testament followers of Yeshua based on what Paul calls "grafting." If you have ever been around a garden which utilizes the horticultural practice of grafting, you will understand the principle in this passage of which Paul is speaking. The native tree would be the Hebrew people and the wild tree or branch would be the Greeks (you and me who are non-Jewish). Jesus died for all mankind, Jewish and Greek. We know this and confirm this based on John 3:16-18. Jesus came to provide a sacrifice for all people, Jewish and Greek.

I am not going to go into depth about the life of Moses, I have already provided an overview of his main accomplishments. Rather, I want to focus on the final conversation he had with God which is found in the book of Deuteronomy. God had walked with Moses all these many years, preparing him as a child, and as a man in the wilderness, to come back to Egypt and lead His nation, His covenant people, out of bondage. The plan was to bring the Hebrew nation into a promised land, a land which He promised Abraham's descendants (Genesis 15). What could have been a short trip, turned into 40 years of raising up a new leadership who would go into the Promised Land and conquer it!

Adonai provided Moses with a strategy to surveille the land He promised them (Numbers 13). As is typical of Adonai, He does not need big numbers of faithful, believing people. In this example, Adonai instructed Moses to send out spies, two men from each tribe: a prince, and a support person from each tribe (two are better than one!). Of all the spies sent out, only two (Joshua and Caleb) came back with a positive report of, *"The land through which we passed is an exceptionally good land! Adonai is with us!"* (Full report Numbers 14.)

Their report caused such a stir that those who heard it wanted to stone Joshua and Caleb. Many wanted to assign a new leader who would lead those who wanted to return to Egypt.

Can you imagine having witnessed the miracles of God in the desert, the daily provision of manna, the provision of water for everyone and their animals, the cloud of protection by day and the pillar of fire's warmth at night, the presence of God, the protection from Pharaoh's army, the dividing of the waters and the complete annihilation of Pharaoh's army, all the instructions given by Adonai of the Tent of Meeting, its furnishing and uses, and the giving of the Ten Commandments? And now they turn on the spies because of their fear of the enemies in their land?

Adonai saw this behavior as a personal affront and wanted to kill them all. They were spared by Moses talking Adonai down from His anger (Numbers 14:20-45). It was unbelief which kept an entire generation from entering the promised land.

CHOOSE LIFE!

So here is the final instructional conversation between Adonai and Moses. It sounds much like the instructions given to New Testament followers of Messiah.

Adonai instructing Moses says,

> I call the heavens and the earth to witness about you today, that I have set before you life and death, the blessing, and the curse. Therefore, **choose life** so that you and your descendants may live, by loving Adonai your God, listening to His voice, and clinging to Him. For **He is your life** and **the length of your days,** that you may dwell on the land that Adonai swore to your fathers—to Abraham, to Isaac and to Jacob —to give them.

Fast forward centuries later and Jesus mirrors His Father's instructions.

Yeshua declared with us what is called, the New Covenant or Commandments recorded in by Matthew,

> You shall love Adonai your God with all your heart, and with all your soul, and with all your mind. This is the first and greatest commandment. And the second is like it, You shall love your neighbor as yourself. The entire Torah and the Prophets hang on these two commandments. (Matthew 22:37-40)

Jesus came to fulfill the Law and in essence, He pared the original Ten Commandments down to two, these being the greatest of them all.

Don't the original Commandments sound strikingly like the declaration of Jesus?

As New Testament followers of Jesus, we have the same choice as did the early followers of Adonai. Jesus said of Himself, "I am the way, the truth, and the life! No one comes to the Father except

80

through Me" (John 14:6).

We have a choice. We can listen to and follow Jesus, or we can ignore His instruction and suffer the consequences which the Hebrew nation suffered.

It is my hope that through the study of the Bible, through the Choose Life Journal plan, you will come to the knowledge of Jesus the Messiah, and you will place your faith and trust in Him alone. I hope you will make this spiritual journey with Jesus, a lifetime commitment and lifestyle. By choosing Jesus, you are choosing life, eternal life.

First Place Ministries wants to walk this Choose Life journey with you. We send out a journal entry every day as an example of what your journaling experience can look like. We seek to provide inspiration to keep you on the journey with Adonai and to persevere during the tough days.

We hope you will use the PRAAYER acronym as a template in guiding you through the process of writing out your personal journal each day. Remember, your journal will be a testimony of your journey with God to your children and their children for generations to come. For as long as Jesus tarries, your testimony of faith will live on beyond your days. Your testimony of faith documented in your journal, becomes your historical record of faith!

Remember to Choose Life! It is your choice and is a decision which affects future generations! Choose Life is so that you and your descendants may live! The choice is yours!

If you are not receiving our Choose Life Journal daily, please go to *www.firstplaceministries.com* and subscribe with your name and email address. You may also download the Choose Life app from your phone's app store.

FOR GROUP DISCUSSION

1. How pivotal was the conversation between Adonai and Moses to the transition of the Hebrew nation, in coming into a new land?

2. How important is the journaling process to your journey with God? How important could it be for your children to see your faith documented?

3. Have you made the choice to Choose Life in Jesus? Have you made your decision public? Please share your decision with your group.

4. Write out your declaration to commit to the Choose Life Journal plan in the space below. The power of this process is the daily action statement you make as a commitment between you and God. (James 1:22) "But be doers of the Word, and not hearers only, deluding yourselves."

Why I like the Tree of Life Version of the Bible

Proverbs 3:18: *She (wisdom) is a tree of life to those who embrace her and blessed will be all who hold firmly to her.*

Proverbs 11:30: *The fruit of the righteous is a tree of life, and whoever wins souls is wise.*

Proverbs 13:1: *Hope deferred makes the heart sick, but a longing fulfilled is a tree of life.*

Proverbs 15:4: *A healing tongue is a tree of life, but a deceitful one crushes the spirit.*

Revelation 2:7b: *To the one who overcomes, I will grant the right to eat from the Tree of Life which is in the Paradise of God.*

Revelation 22:2b: *On either side of the river was a tree of life, bearing twelve kinds of fruit, yielding its fruit each month; and the leaves of the tree were for the healing of the nations.*

Revelation 22:14: *How fortunate are those who wash their robes, so that they may have the right to the Tree of Life and may enter through the gates into the city.*

Revelation 22:18-19: *I testify to everyone who hears the words of the prophecy of this book. If anyone adds to them, God shall add to him the plagues that are written in this book, and if anyone takes away from the words of the book of this prophecy, God shall take away his share in the Tree of Life and the Holy City, which are written in this book.*

I like the Tree of Life Version (TLV) because of the Jewishness of its content. This version intentionally sets out to break traditional English versions and dared to substitute Hebrew terms for:

God:	*Adonai Elyon*
Jesus:	*Yeshua Messiah*
Holy Spirit:	*Ruach*
Holy days:	*kadosh*
Festivals:	ex. *Sukkot*

and a host of other traditional Jewish terms like

saints, holy ones:	*kedoshim*
peace:	*shalom*
blessings:	*bracha*
save now:	*hoshia-na*

Knowing and using these terms shines new light on the gospel and new understanding. My last example, *"hoshia-na"* (our hosanna), came to life this past year in a study of the gospels (Matthew 21:9, Mark 11:9-10, John 12:13), where I discovered that the meaning of *"hoshia-na"* is "save now" or "please save."

The people observing Yeshua's entry into Jerusalem were not only cheering, as we preach and portray in our plays and pageants, they were crying out in earnest, "Save us now!" They had experienced enough oppression at the hands of the Roman soldiers, and perhaps they had suffered long enough at the hands of the Pharisees, Sadducees, and the Sanhedrin.

Oppression is not an exclusive trait of governments. Matthew, Mark, and Luke each mention the abuse of widows: *"They devour widows' houses and make long prayers as a show"* (Luke 20:47).

Do you think the gospel writers were referring to legislators? I suppose some could be guilty of "long prayers," but Luke clearly accuses the religious leaders of his time as being the culprits.

Isaiah, on the other hand, also says,

> *Oy (Woe) to those enacting unjust decrees and recording corrupt legislation, to deprive the helpless of justice and rob the rights of the poor of My people so that widows may be their spoil and orphans their prey! What will you do on the day of visitation, when desolation comes from afar? To whom will you flee for help? Where will you leave your wealth?*

I had an experience about five years ago that I will never forget. A widow from the East coast contacted me through The Widows Project. She had a home that was in foreclosure, and she had equity. I made several phone calls to pastors in the area, trying to locate legal help. I did not receive one call from anyone in her area who was willing to help this woman. She had a business too, which was in trouble as well. I believe that with the equity she claimed she had, she could have qualified for a reverse mortgage, saved her home and her equity. She was victimized by predatory lenders.

Preying on the widowed and orphans is not a new concept and has existed both today as well as in the governing powers and the religious community in the Bible.

I also like that the translators of the TLV Bible used the term *"communities"* instead of *"church."* They more accurately translated the Greek term *"Ekklesia,"* which means he called out and "a ruling, governing body." This discovery of Matthew 16:18, where Jesus declares to Peter, "Upon this rock I will build My community," is more accurate to the text. The word "church" had not even been invented yet by any language. Its roots come from the German "kirche."

We fail to realize that the new community of faith was establishing a new identity for the followers of Yeshua. They were breaking away from the religious traditions of the Torah (Law) and its rules, like circumcision. The Jewish side wanted to impose the laws of its faith upon the Greeks (us). We still experience the same battles today over Charisma and non-Charisma and End Times Theology. How much simpler can we get than to embrace the Apostolic model and the Apostles Creed?

We all want to argue that the Apostolic age is over but consider how much simpler it was. The problem is man. Rather than embrace a Theocratic model, we like to create titles, denominational names and distinctives, and argue about the non-essential.

Here is how Paul sums it up to a young Timothy:

Trustworthy is the saying: If we died with Him, we will also live with Him; if we endure, we will also reign with Him; if we deny Him, He will also deny us; if we are faithless, He remains faithful, for He cannot deny Himself. Remind them of these things and solemnly charge them before God not to quarrel about words, which is useless—to the ruin of those who are listening. Make every effort to present yourself before God as tried and true, as an unashamed worker cutting a straight path with the Word of truth. But avoid godless chatter, for it will lead to further ungodliness and their words will spread like cancer. Among them are Hymenaeus and Philetus—men who have missed the mark concerning the truth, saying that the resurrection has already taken place. They are overturning the faith of some. Nevertheless, the firm foundation of God stands, having this seal: "The Lord knows those who are His," and "Let everyone who names the name of the Lord keep away from unrighteousness."

Now in a great house, there are not only vessels of gold and silver but also of wood and clay—some for honor and some for common use. Therefore, if anyone cleanses himself from these, he will be a vessel for honor—sanctified, useful to the Master, prepared for every good work. 2 Timothy 2:11-21

Paul also emphasizes the issue in Titus 3:9: *"But avoid foolish controversies and genealogies and strife and disputes about Torah, for they are unprofitable and useless."*

Are these foolish controversies and disputes really worth it? Do they accomplish God's work? Or do they just implicate us all? I am guilty if I perpetuate the non-truth of most translations.

I also like the TLV because it more accurately conveys the subtle distinctive difference in the Greek word, *"doulos"* meaning either slave or servant. Most translations, including the King James, use the word "servant." The TLV correctly uses the word "slave." I wrote on this topic in my last book, **BONDSLAVE: The Inconvenient Truth About Your Identity in Christ.**

My conviction is that Paul was talking about being a "slave" of Yeshua when he lists to the Corinthians all the suffering he has experienced. Do servants endure prison, beatings, forty lashes minus one (five separate times), stoning, three shipwrecks, danger from floods and robbers, danger at sea, sleepless nights, hunger, and thirst, cold and exposure? I do not believe so. After all, the Lord prophesied that he was going to show Paul how much he must *"suffer for My name's sake"* (Acts 9:16).

In Romans 6, Paul is abundantly clear that he is talking about spiritual slavery. We once were "slaves to sin," but now you are "slaves to righteousness." How many pastors have told you this? Few, because it is not politically correct to talk about slavery in any form today. It may not be popular, but it is the truth. We are slaves to that which we obey. Paul encourages us to be *"set free from sin and having become enslaved to God, you have your fruit resulting in holiness. And the outcome is eternal life"* (vs. 22). I encourage you to become and identify as a bondslave of Yeshua Messiah!

Just as an aside, I believe that King James (I do not respect him any more than I respect satan) also had the Greek term *"doulos"* translated as *servant* for this reason. What was the primary financial mechanism in his country? Slavery. He did not want to disparage that which he was involved in.

Man oppresses and Yeshua frees. We have seen it throughout history. Yeshua intimately understands man's heart. We like to say,

"They are good people." Adonai says:

> the heart is deceitful above all things, and incurable (it is redeemable though)—who can know it? I, Adonai, search the heart; I try the mind, to give every man according to his ways, according to his deeds (Jeremiah 17:9-10).

I should add that I do not hold King James as singularly responsible. There are 47 theologians who are culpable. I am personally concerned for their souls. They knowingly bowed to the king's wishes and were disobedient to the King of Kings. There are consequences to their actions explained in Revelation 22:18b-19:

> I testify to everyone who hears the words of the prophecy of this book. If anyone adds to them, God shall add to him the plagues that are written in this book; and if anyone takes away from the words of the book of this prophecy, God shall take away his share in the Tree of Life and the Holy City, which are written in this book.

Let us *not* continue to perpetuate a lie.

I want to quote Dr. Jeffrey L. Seif, Tanakh Project Manager and Vice President:

> We believe that reckonings of Hebrew, Aramaic, and Greek manuscripts have all too often been tendered by churchmen with little to no intellectual interest in the Jewish experience, no emotional connection to the Jewish people, and no real personal support for the Jewish homeland—Israel. The upshot of the disregard, be it intentional or accidental, is that biblical books that were written to Jews, for Jews, and about Jews lose a critical element—their actual Jewish essence. Readers wanting to come to terms with the Bible's messages, messengers, and recipients are thus all too easily directed away from the main Author's storylines and intents. Jewish displacement and replacement motifs come through in ways that are subtle and in ways that are not so subtle. Either way, and the translator's intentions aside, God's will and ways can be obscured through their jaded bias. The result is that anti-biblical prejudice germinates, the anti-biblical soul sickness inadvertently passes on to the next generation of Bible readers, and the world all too easily suffers the loss of a vision of What God is up to in His Word and in His world. (pg. X, TLV Bible)

He is absolutely correct. This has gone on for generations, being handed down as gospel and the only true authority. I unapologetically say that I can no longer support the institution of church, and in my book *Ekklesia Declared*, I outline the historical reasons for my position.

I am cautious about the King James Version of the Bible. The king had an objective and he succeeded in controlling his kingdom. That control has reached across the seas and subjected many to a man-made, religious culture—one in which he tried to usurp the true Head of his bride, Yeshua. He is like his father who also tried to usurp the God (Elohim), the true Sovereign of heaven and earth.

I declare that there is only one true Sovereign, and it is not King James.

How Will They Know If We Won't Go?

By Joe Monroe, (Used with permission)

The five guys of our incognito missionary SPRINT team had access to complementary bike transportation along with our hotel room rental in Guangzhou, China.

Back in the summer of 1984, we were a total of ten students, five guys and five young women. We were to be the first of many overseas student mission teams sent out by Seattle Pacific University's "Seattle Pacific Reachout International" or "SPRINT" for short.

Nine of us were to venture to Hong Kong under the leadership of a fellow SPU student who also happened to be a Chinese Hong Kong citizen. His passion for the people of Hong Kong, along with the inspiration of a Keith Green video, "Jesus Commands Us to Go," lit the fire in my friend Ray's heart. It was in large part this video that inspired Ray and all nine of us to join him as SPU's first volunteer short-term overseas summer missionary team.

Over the course of two to three quarters, Ray organized the trip and managed to help us raise the funds and support we needed. Ray also made contacts with ministries across the Pacific in his parents' homeland, Hong Kong, and helped us to get full accommodations. We were to spend seven weeks overseas.

The first three weeks were spent working with the Hong Kong Bible Seminary in Kowloon Tong. We were to help teach English during their summertime kids' camp.

The following three weeks were spent working with Hong Kong Youth for Christ.

Our team worked together with these awesome YFC brothers and sisters in Jesus to help assist them to bring the Gospel of Christ to the very young and old. We accomplished this through various events such as street evangelism, and random door to door visits with the "American Christians."

We were, however, not the only short-term missionary team

from a USA Christian University sent to assist the highly organized and brilliant Hong Kong Youth For Christ organization. At least two other Youth With A Mission, or YWAM missionary teams from other Christian Universities from the states were there as well to assist during the summer months.

The culminating YFC event took place in a public park in Hong Kong with Chinese Christian musicians and singers plus testimonials and a proclamation of the Gospel in Cantonese. Something like over five hundred adult listeners and many children joined us on a Saturday afternoon and evening to listen to the gospel of Christ proclaimed under and around a huge tent.

The theme of the three-week ministry series was printed on all our T-shirts. It was a question written in both Chinese and in English asking, "Where Then Is My Home?"

For some context, it is important to note that this was during the time period that Great Britain was getting ready to cede control of the British run territory of Hong Kong to The Peoples Republic of China. To be very clear, it is important to understand this meant in a very real sense, that a democratically free people were now being required to submit and surrender their social, economic, political, and religious freedoms to an authoritarian state.

No one was certain how long the Chinese Communists promise for an autonomous, independent, and economically and religiously free Hong Kong would last.

The peoples of Hong Kong were descendants from many nations, with Hong Kong-raised Chinese, mainland Chinese dissidents (who had fled from a tyrannical communist government), people of various European countries of origin and descent, plus may others from impoverished Asian nations and the Philippine Islands who had fled to this land of opportunity under this British dependent territory.

These people of many differing religions and indeed, even secular walks of life were now very worried and afraid with really no idea how they would adjust to these new authoritarian rulers, the Chinese Communist Government.

Many Christians were also concerned, especially those who had escaped from religious persecution or had already served prison time in Mainland China.

It was also during this final week of our city-wide ministry with Youth For Christ, that we were granted the privilege to tour and visit Hong Kong Bible Radio Station.

Hong Kong Bible Radio Station had a huge tower antenna that was used to pierce the red iron curtain of Mainland Communist China where millions of attendees of underground home churches would tune in to God's Word spoken over their radios.

It was here at Hong Kong Bible Radio Station that each of us young men and young women from our SPRINT team were about to be tasked with what we would later look back on as the first of a series of God Ordained Happenstances.

When Ray let our hosts at the radio station know that we were planning a trip into mainland China that very next week, we were then asked if we each would be willing to carry two or three Bibles into Guangzhou China. We all jumped at the chance at this new adventure.

We were to hand deliver these new Bible translations to any Chinese national Christian who would be interested in owning one.

The caveat in our favor was that these Bibles were written both in the English Language along with a Chinese translation on the opposite page purposely so that the nationals could learn to read English.

In the Eighties, China was very keen on the idea of having their college students learn English.

Hong Kong Bible Radio Station had been beaming in the Word of God by radio for decades.

Many people were hungry in China for the Word of God, and this was a great opportunity to share both the written English language plus the written Word of God, the latter outlawed, but the former encouraged.

The Chinese Communist government encouraged students to speak and write in the English language to help them secure technology and gain an economic edge over their Western adversaries.

These "English language teaching books" came in very handy for us as incognito missionaries while passing through Chinese customs. On our way through customs one of our young ladies in the group was stopped by a People's Liberation Army Soldier before entering Mainland China.

Our young lady explained to the soldier that it was a book, "to help Chinese students to learn English."

After a tense ten minutes, the soldier's commanding officer stepped in to take over. After thumbing through the "English language teaching book," and turning it upside down to shake lose any contraband, the commanding officer handed the Bible back to our young lady and proceeded to wave her and all the rest of our team through, thereby alleviating the fear of us Americans being detained, and worse, the threat of our friend and leader Ray being sent off to a Chinese prison camp.

The heat in the Guangzhou China sun, in combination with the high humidity, was nearly unbearable during the day reaching into the high 90's Fahrenheit.

Our hot daily schedule included tour-guide-led bus and walking tours to various temples, pottery factories, and other Chinese cultural locations.

At such places, we were allowed to speak with certain locals that we suspected were trained to speak to tourists, never uttering anything negative about the Chinese Dictatorship.

Along with chit chat about the fantastic Chinese culture of the past, there was a lot of propaganda spoken to us about how wonderfully forward, modern, and advanced China had become since the People's Revolution.

Most importantly, it was consistently impressed upon us how the Chinese people were exceedingly grateful to the People's Republic for providing for the health and welfare of all of China's citizens, and how so many had come to benefit financially from this great Utopian Society.

It seemed at times like we were in Chinese Disney Land, where everything was carefully scripted and orchestrated. It was, however, very obvious to all of us that things were pretty Mickey Mouse and very fake.

This façade was easily called into question when we could look just a short distance of maybe 50 yards across a bridge from our location on the peninsula.

Just across the river that separated the beautifully green and lush peninsula where our modest hotel was located, along with a grand 5-star hotel where President Ronald Reagan once stayed, was constructed a very conspicuous plywood, cardboard, and blue tarp shanty town on a mud flat.

Once, we had tried to cross this bridge during the day, chatting it up with several of the young People's Liberation Army soldiers who stood guard, allowing only certain uniformed workers to cross.

We had a plan to perhaps buddy-up to the guards and hopefully get a pass to cross over and talk with "the real locals" on the other side of the bridge.

Things, however, did not quite go as we had imagined.

One of our guys tried to make his move by moseying just a yard or two onto the bridge for a photo opportunity.

Pantomime and laughter turned to stern faces and a shoulder-to-shoulder formation of a human wall that blocked our pathway.

Our friend was immediately persuaded by the armed soldiers that he should turn back.

Once our fellow partner came back to the safe zone, all smiles returned again to both groups.

It was only at night that one felt great relief from the heat of the day, and from the press of the hurried people and the ever-watchful eye of an armed soldier.

Finally, about halfway through our week stay in China, the hot nighttime temperatures broke, with perhaps a ten degree drop. We men decided we could finally take an opportunity for a guys' night out on the town via our free bicycle transportation.

For some reason, the soldiers were out in less force the night we took our bike ride, allowing us an advantage to venture a little closer to the "real local folks" of Guangzhou China.

This was to be the second God-ordained happenstance.

When our group had ridden about ten minutes from our hotel, we rounded the corner of the street we were traveling and noticed a huge three-story white Victorian era house with a wraparound porch, lit brightly with Chinese lanterns hanging from the eaves and electric chandeliers hanging inside, along with masses of people seemingly partying, and sitting around tables, but without any band music.

As we approached, I was in awe of how many people continued to pour in and out of the house, which in fact was not a home at all, but a Chinese ice cream parlor.

When the five of us entered, nearly every table was full, with the exception of one. The two gentlemen seated at that table looked up, met our foreign eyes, and immediately stood up and offered for us to join them.

Excitedly, one man interpreted for his friend in Mandarin as he spoke to us in excellent English. He had learned English as a young boy in school in China, which ensured him a position working with English-speaking travelers.

It wouldn't be until later that we learned that the Chinese Communist government made the decision for the Chinese children as to what their careers would be, based on their various, carefully government-crafted skills.

At first, all questions were directed toward us. "Where in the USA are you from? What occupation do you have? Have you family?"

When it was discovered that we were all American students from Seattle Pacific University visiting China on holiday, both men became quite fascinated that we were allowed in our country to choose for ourselves our own majors and therefore our own direction in what occupations we could pursue.

Such freedom of occupational choice was unheard of and sounded too fantastic to believe to these men. They were even more astonished that the university we attended was a Christian University.

How could such a thing exist?

To these men, it made no sense. The Chinese government had convinced their people that although we were a selfish nation caring only about comfort, money, and world domination, we were at least advanced enough to no longer believe in religious fairy tales.

When we explained that their understanding of American religion was incorrect, and that, in fact, the predominant religion in the USA was Christianity, and the fact that many Christian universities exist to train highly skilled businessmen, doctors, lawyers, teachers and even actors and ministers to spread the Gospel of Christ and to help our fellow men and women in all of life's circumstances, they became animated and very happily excited.

"We never knew this! We have only heard about this God over Hong Kong Bible Radio Station! Please, tell us more!"

This epiphany for them resulted in an invitation by us to come back to our hotel room where we could speak more freely and confidentiality.

Our new Chinese English-speaking friend excitedly translated our invitation to his buddy and together they immediately rose from their seats and said, "Alright! Let's go now!"

Being, however, the selfish Americans we were initially perceived as, we asked for permission to first finish our ice cream, for which they happily and patiently obliged.

Back at our hotel room, it was explained that one of our guys was a Biblical Studies Major. Again, they were astonished, "You believe this Bible?"

We each took some time to give our testimonies. Once finished, we explained that for us, this was not just a religion but a way of fulfillment, happiness and meaning for our existence. This was an ever-growing relationship with our creator. A few more questions of how and why we came to believe in Jesus followed.

Then our new friend and interpreter asked us, "Do you have this Bible?"

"As a matter of fact, we do," said one of our guys.

"Yes, we do!" I chimed in. "In fact, we brought some printed in both the Chinese and English languages. Would you guys like them?"

It was the best gift reception I had ever witnessed! Even beyond the excitement of little kids receiving a brand-new bike on Christmas morning.

Smiles, tears, and laughter, along with many handshakes, happened after the presentation of the gifts of their new Bibles. When all was calm, our interpreter friend exchanged words with his buddy and then he proceeded to translate.

"This is so very much appreciated! We have been hearing about this God, and about His Word written in a book called the Bible, over Hong Kong Bible Radio Station for five years! And we have always been asking and praying to this God, that if You are real, please send us Bibles! And today it has become true!"

It was then our turn to become astounded and excited and a bit awestruck. The final happenstance had occurred. The Most High God had heard their prayers and even more so, honored their fervent consistent pleas for five whole years, and He chose this day for us to have the privilege of being the carriers of His Word, to their hands.

These series of events weren't just happenstances. These were miraculous signs and wonders from a Heavenly Father who had heard and answered their fervent prayers with a greater love than either of them had ever experienced.

It amazes me to this day. Even after experiencing so great a miracle as this, I allow work and play and existence to get in the way of experiencing true life by sitting down regularly and reading and feasting upon God's Word.

This event occurred over 30 years ago. I cannot imagine two men waiting so patiently and for five years, consistently asking God for His Living Word to come to them, only to allow their Bibles to sit on a desktop gathering dust.

God has promised to give us "Life", and that Life so much more abundantly! Although we as Americans may claim to "know God", how can we truly know and experience the only loving and Most High Heavenly Father God without spending time being mentored by His Holy Spirit through His Living Word?

After giving our new friends their Bibles, it was time for us to learn about them.

"What do you two do for work in China?", one of our guys asked.

"Oh, yes! We work in (National Security for the Chinese Government)!"

We all were shaken. What? How? Were we about to be arrested? Our friend Ray had the blood drain from his face, and he very nearly passed out from fear of being sent to a Chinese prison!

They both immediately recognized the fear on all of our faces and said, "No, no, no! Please do not worry! Although our work was chosen for us, we do NOT believe our government! So many lies for so long a time! Most of the Chinese students at University do not believe the government lies anymore. And now we know this God we have heard about over Hong Kong Bible Radio Station is real!"

As a footnote, it was in Tiananmen Square, Beijing, April 15 of 1989, five years later, that a student uprising and demonstration of Chinese students' displeasure with the rule of The People's Republic of China began. The students had become disillusioned with communism and were seeking democracy. They were forcibly suppressed when the government declared martial law on June 14th and sent The Peoples Liberation Army with tanks and automatic rifles. Estimates of the death toll vary from several hundred to several thousand, with thousands more wounded. We may never know the true numbers, just as we may never know the true numbers of the growth of God's Holy Spirit in the hearts of so many of the Chinese people who were so willing to acquire, read, listen, and understand His Word, despite the threat of five years imprisonment and or even death.

THE BOOK OF JOHN

CHOOSE LIFE JOURNAL 21-DAY START

We have created additional resources to assist your study of the Word.

On our website, www.firstplaceministries.com you can:

- subscribe to receive the Choose Life Journal daily via email,

- access the reading schedule (under the Tools tab), and

- print a copy of the Choose Life Journal template.

We also encourage you to download our Choose Life Journal phone app, available free from your app store. No matter where you are, you will have unlimited access to the Choose Life Journal, reading schedule, and the Tree of Life Bible version in the palm of your hand.

For more information, please reference Chapter 7: Guidelines for Launching a New Lifestyle of Journaling Time with God.

Choose Life Journal

DATE: TITLE:

PRAYER:

READING:

ATTENTION:

ACTION:

YIELD:

ENGAGE:

RESPONSE:

MEMORY VERSE:

MUSIC

JOHN 1

Prayer: Father, I ask for those who are choosing to engage with the Choose Life Journal, that you will help them develop the desire and discipline to develop a lifestyle of daily feeding themselves with the Bread of Life! May they hunger and thirst for righteousness. In Jesus' name, amen.

Reading: John 1:19-23

> *¹⁹ This is John's testimony, when the Judean leaders sent kohanim and Levites from Jerusalem to ask him, "Who are you?"*
> *²⁰ He openly admitted and did not deny; he admitted, "I am not the Messiah."*
> *²¹ "What then? Are you Elijah?" they asked him.*
> *"I am not," said John.*
> *"Are you the Prophet?"*
> *"No," he answered.*
> *²² So they said to him, "Who are you? Give us an answer for those who sent us. What do you say about yourself?"*
> *²³ He said, "I am 'the voice of one crying in the wilderness, "Make straight the way of ADONAI,"' as the prophet Isaiah said."*

Attention: Knowing who you are is a critical part of life, especially your spiritual life. John knew who he was. He knew his purpose: To point people to Jesus as the Messiah. As New Testament followers of Jesus, we too are His voice, His messengers.

Do you know your purpose? Do you strive to fulfill your purpose on earth? If you are a follower of Jesus, He left all followers a message, a mandate before He ascended into Heaven.

Matthew 28:18-20 gives the follower of Jesus His purpose for our lives.

> *All authority in heaven and on earth has been given to Me. Go therefore and make disciples of all nations, immersing them in the name of the Father and the Son and the Ruach ha Kodesh, teaching them to observe all I have commanded you. And*

remember! I am with you always, even to the end of the age.

Some of us have heeded the command to "go". Some have baptized. But sadly, we have done a poor job of discipling people. Discipling takes time and energy and is a slow, daily process. Discipling is what our "Daily Choose Life Study and Journaling" is all about. You are being discipled and mentored in the things of God, Jesus and the Holy Spirit. You may find it a struggle to accomplish a daily time in the Word. Why? Because this daily lifestyle takes intentional discipline to accomplish.

Do you remember as a child your mother reminding you to brush your teeth before you went to bed? How many times did she have to remind you?

I am your daily reminder, encourager and mentor. I have been doing this for over 15 years. My day is not complete without spending time with Jesus. I encourage you to intentionally do the same.

We have an app now which will help you access the Choose Life Journal from the palm of your hand. Just download the app and enjoy access any time of the day.

If you haven't been born again, the study of John will share with you how to receive Jesus, be water baptized, follow Jesus, and be immersed in His Spirit.

Please email me: *Rolland@firstplaceministries.com* if you have asked Jesus into your heart or if you desire to know Him. I'd love to pray for you, with you, and encourage you in the process of daily walking with Jesus. I invite all people that are engaging in the daily Choose Life process to point people to Jesus by sharing your testimony and/or touching their life through an act of service.

Action: I will prayerfully seek to touch others and point them to Jesus today and tomorrow, forever.

Yield: A yielded life is a fulfilling life!

Engage: An engaged life is a purposeful life!

Responding: A responding life is a relationally purposeful life with Jesus and people.

Prayer: Father, what a way to start a new year! What a way to begin anew and afresh with You by being in the Word daily and processing life with You! You give meaning and purpose to my life! I am so grateful for Jesus! Amen.

Memory Scripture of the Day: John 1:29b

Behold, the Lamb of God who takes away the sin of the world!

Music: John 1:1-5 In the beginning was the Word – performed by the CBU University Choir and Orchestra

Remember, abide in Jesus today.

JOHN 2

Prayer: Father, may I see new truths in Your Word today. Help me to seek You, the One who did the miracles rather than the miracles. May we all seek the Miracle Worker! In Jesus' name, amen!

Reading: John 2 focus: v18-21

> *¹⁸ The Judean leaders responded, "What sign do You show us, since You are doing these things?"*
>
> *¹⁹ "Destroy this Temple," Yeshua answered them, "and in three days I will raise it up."*
>
> *²⁰ The Judean leaders then said to Him, "Forty-six years this Temple was being built, and You will raise it up in three days?" ²¹ But He was talking about the temple of His body. ²² So after He was raised from the dead, His disciples remembered that He was talking about this. Then they believed the Scripture and the Word that Yeshua had spoken.*

Attention: Every miracle that Jesus performed was intentional and for the purpose of glorifying His Father and building belief in His disciples. Each of the two miracles in this chapter (making wine from water and purging the Temple) resulted in *"He revealed His glory, and His disciples believed in Him"* (vs. 11), and *"...many believed in His name, seeing the signs He was doing"* (vs. 23).

Many sought a sign. Many today seek a sign and not the miracle or Sign Maker. Are you guilty of seeking the sign or miracle, more than wanting Jesus?

John recorded Jesus saying (20:29):

> *"Blessed are the ones who have not seen and yet believe."* Are you blessed with believing without seeing? Or have you seen and don't believe? I encourage you today to *"believe (put your trust) in the Lord Jesus Christ (Yeshua) and you will be saved— you and your household"* (16:31).

Action: Jesus I place my complete trust in You to save me and my household! I claim my family for Your Kingdom!

Yield: Will you yield to Jesus today and for every day forward?

Engage: I will engage in a lifestyle pleasing to Jesus today!

Relationship: I choose life in Jesus today! My relationship with Jesus changes everything because it changes me!

Prayer: Jesus, I can't imagine life without You. I've tried living my own life under my control and decision making and failed miserably. I entrust my life to You today and every day forward! Be the pilot of my life! In Jesus' name. Amen.

Memory verse today: John 2:11b

He revealed His glory, and His disciples believed in Him.

Music: Natalie Grant – More Than Anything

Remember, abide in Jesus today.

JOHN 3

Prayer: Father I ask for understanding today about being "born of water and spirit." May Your Holy Spirit help me to clarify and make simple, that which we make so difficult. I yield my mind, my heart and spirit to You. In Jesus' name. Amen.

Reading: John 3 focal point: vs 3, 5-6

> *³ Yeshua answered him, "Amen, amen I tell you, unless one is born from above he cannot see the kingdom of God."*

> *⁵ Yeshua answered, "Amen, amen I tell you, unless one is born of water and spirit he cannot enter the kingdom of God. ⁶ What is born of the flesh is flesh, and what is born of the Spirit is spirit.*

Attention: John allows us to listen in on a conversation between Nicodemus and Yeshua (Jesus). Understanding who Nicodemus is makes this conversation meaningful. John identifies Nicodemus as a Pharisee, "a ruler of the Jews" (John 3:1), that is, a member of the Sanhedrin, the Jewish ruling council, and as "a teacher of Israel" (John 3:10), that is, an authority on the interpretation of the Hebrew Scriptures (Holman Illustrated Bible Dictionary). We are not told whether Nicodemus, who chose to come to see Jesus at night (so he wouldn't be recognized?), becomes born again but we do see Nicodemus after Jesus' death publicly participating in the burial preparation. He brought "about a hundred pounds of myrrh and aloes" (John 19:39).

I recall as a 9-year-old boy, a pastor sharing with me how to be born again. He pulled a dime out of his pocket and told me, "If I was to give this dime to you as a gift, what would you have to do to receive it." He said, "you would have to reach out and accept or receive it, wouldn't you?" I had to claim the gift, as my own. The only action on our part is to receive what God has offered each one of us in the gift of Jesus.

This act of servanthood by Nicodemus would seem to indicate that he came to understand the act of being born again. While he initially came to Jesus at night, he came publicly to anoint His body. There is no such thing as secret disciple. If you have trusted Jesus and invited Him to be the Lord and King of your heart, tell somebody what you have transacted with Jesus. It is the greatest decision you will ever make!

Action: Jesus, I invite you to be Lord of my life!

Yield: Surrender your heart to Jesus. There is no greater way to say I love You Jesus.

Engage: Intentionally engage in meeting with other followers of Jesus!

Reconciliation: Must happen with God before it can happen with others!

Prayer: Father, with the start of a new year, what a time to begin following You! I pray for every person receiving this email. I claim them for Your kingdom. May they become born again, born of water and spirit. May they seek to be water baptized if they have experienced new birth. I invite every person to rededicate and yield themselves to You Jesus. May '21 be a year of dynamic spiritual growth in all of us! In Jesus' name. Amen!

Memory verse: John 3:16

> [16] *"For God so loved the world that He gave His one and only Son, that whoever believes in Him shall not perish but have eternal life.*

Music: God so loved the world

Remember, abide in Jesus today.

JOHN 4

Prayer: Father, I pray that each person will see today, that they are significant. They are vital and important in the eyes of family and friends. Reveal Yourself to each person today. In Jesus' name. Amen.

Reading: John 4 focal vs. 46b-47

> *"Now there was a nobleman whose son was sick in Capernaum. When he heard that Yeshua (Jesus) had come from Judea to the Galilee, he went to Him and begged Him to come down and heal his son; for he was about to die. The nobleman said to Him, 'Sir, come down before my child dies!' Yeshua tells him, '***Go! Your son lives!***' The man believed the Word that Yeshua said to him and started off."*

Attention: Have you ever had a family member that you have "contended" for with Jesus? Your son or daughter is gravely ill, or is not walking with Jesus and strung out on drugs? This was a life-or-death matter that was urgent to the man. He cared desperately for his son. He appealed for Jesus to come to his son's bedside. The word Jesus gives him, "Go! Your son lives!"

We are told that this man started off for home, satisfied with Jesus' response that his son "lives!" If we received that word about our son, would we "believe" and return home in faith?"

I want to emphasize vs.51-53. John tells us that while on his way home, the man was met by his servants. With curiosity, the nobleman asks his servants, "When did the boy begin to get better?" They said, "The fever left him yesterday at about the seventh hour." Then the father realized that it was the same hour Yeshua said to him, "Your son lives!" Now he himself believed, along with his whole household."

I share this passage to underscore your importance to your family or those around you. You matter! In many cultures and even those in biblical times, when the father believed, so did the whole household. As the father believes, his wife and children follow. You are the key to your children's spiritual future. (If you want more proof, read Acts 16:30-34.)

Action: I will follow You, Jesus, because I see that I am the key factor in my family following You.

Yielded: Father, my life is yielded to You!

Engage: Jesus, I will spend time daily with You because my children will see and I will be prepared to share with them.

Relationship: Father, I see that my relationship with You influences my children and wife.

Memory verse: John 5:53b

*Now he himself **believed**, along with his whole household.*

Remember, abide in Jesus today.

JOHN 5

Prayer: Father, I feel the acceleration of end time events happening all around us. Just as those events are accelerating, I ask that You accelerate Your events in our lives. May we give witness to same-day healings and miracles. May we see multiplication of our efforts in ministry of salvations, healings, reconciliations, restoration of relationships, creation of resources (in discipleship, mentoring, support groups, apps), new leadership, and financial provision. Amen.

Reading: John 5 Focus: vs.5-10

> *"Now a certain man had been an invalid there for **thirty-eight years.** Seeing him lying there and knowing he had been that way a long time, Yeshua said to him, 'Do you want to get well?' The invalid answered Him, 'Sir, I have nobody to put me into the pool when the water is stirred up. While I'm trying to get in, somebody else steps down before me!' Yeshua tells him, 'Get up! Pick up your mat and walk!'*
>
> *Immediately, the man was healed! He took us his mat and started walking around. Now that day was Shabbat, so Judean leaders were saying to the man who was healed, 'It's Shabbat Sabbath rest)! It's not permitted for you to carry your mat.'"*

Attention: John shares with us an "eyewitness" account of a man who has been an invalid (apparently severely disabled) for 38 years. We are not told the man's age, but we must suspect that his disability had been with him for most of his life. He had perhaps never experienced mobility like most children and adults. He had only viewed life from the ground up and he has a divine encounter with Jesus which we are told, changed everything for him.

Does it seem odd to you that Yeshua (Jesus) asks the man, *"Do you want to get well?"*

I believe this question shows that Jesus won't impose His will on any of us. There may be some who prefer to stay as they are and not want to be healed. Have you ever seen someone who wouldn't change as they were too comfortable with their current situation?

They would say they wanted out but are so encumbered they never change. Or they are addicted and love the addiction even though it is killing them.

The man never answers Jesus. On the face, his response appears more like an excuse. "Sir, I have nobody to put me into the pool." If he truly wanted to be healed, could he have been set right on the pool's edge? Positioned so all he had to do was roll over? All we know is Jesus had compassion on him and healed him.

John uses the word, *"immediately"* to define how the man was "healed." I wonder how many years we have lived with something that has kept us captive? Are we ready to be healed? Or will it take us 30, 40, 50 years to be ready for a divine encounter with Jesus? He is ready whenever we are ready. Could it be today? I want to tell you, being "born again" is a miracle! It is the greatest miracle that Jesus gives us. If you know Jesus as Lord and Savior, do not be guilty of saying, "Jesus has never done a miracle for me." He has done the greatest miracle anyone can do for you. If you know Him and are living for Him, is today the day that you allow Him to do another miracle for you?

Action: Jesus, I am ready to experience a same day miracle in my life. I ask for a miracle in reconciliation with my children. (Be specific with Jesus.)

Yielding: Jesus, I yield my life to You!

Engaging: Jesus, keep me attached and abiding in You!

Restore: unto me the joy of Your salvation. I rejoice today in being reconciled with my children.

Prayer: Jesus, there is no greater miracle than the day You saved me and redeemed me to eternal life with You! Thank You for giving me life and transforming me by renewing my mind and my heart! I praise You Jesus. Amen!

Memory Scripture: (vs.39)

> *You search the Scriptures because you suppose that in them you have eternal life. It is these that testify about Me.*

Music: Jeremy Camp- Dead Man Walking, Gaither Vocal Band: He Touched Me

Remember: Abide in Jesus today.

JOHN 6

Prayer: Father, I ask You to reveal to each person today another nugget of truth about who You are and Your desire for us. May each of us arrive at awareness that You are "life", and Your words are "eternal life". Amen!

Reading: John 6 key: vs. 39-40

> *"Now **this is the will of the One who sent Me**, that I lose not one of all He has given Me, but raise each one on the last day. For **this is the will of My Father**, that everyone who sees the Son and trusts in Him may have eternal life: and I will raise him up on the last day."*

Attention: Have you ever bought something that required you to put it together? Have you ever tried to do it without looking at or reading the directions? How did that work for you? Might I suggest that trying to live life on your own without reading the Bible is like not using the instruction manual? I think all of us that are older would unanimously agree, we crashed and burned. There is a popular talk show psychologist who I have heard say, "How's that working for you?"

I want to share two Scripture references with you that underscore the reason God had the Bible written. One is found in Romans 15:4 and the other in 1 Corinthians 10:6 & 11. I want you to read those two passages and highlight or underline them. They both tell us that the Bible was "written for our instruction", and they bring "hope."

I would encourage over the course of your reading and studying this year, watch for a verse that becomes your own. It is what I call a "life verse." Mine is Acts 17:28b "in Him (Jesus) we live and move and have our being." This verse shares my heart about Jesus. He is my everything! He is the source of my life!

Did you know that God has expressed His will through Jesus? The highlighted Scripture tells us definitively, *"this is the will of My Father!"* This is a twofold will, that "everyone" who "sees the Son and trusts in Him may have eternal life" and will be resurrected "on the last day." Salvation and resurrection are assured for those who have placed their trust in Jesus.

Action: I place my trust in Jesus from this day forward. I will engage in a daily lifestyle of studying and journaling with the Holy Spirit and His Word.

Yielding: is submission to His will and His ways.

Engaging: is daily!

Relationship: is 24/7 I cannot live without Jesus. Apart from Him I am just surviving and not living.

Memory verse: vs 33b-34

> *My Father gives you the true bread from heaven. For the bread of God is the One coming down from heaven and giving life to the world.*

Music video: Keith Green -Your Love Broke Through,

Fred Hammond – Bread of Life

Remember: Abide in Jesus today.

JOHN 7

Prayer: Father, I ask for fresh revelation from Your Holy Spirit. Pour out Your Spirit upon us. Fill us and continue to indwell us. Thank You for the living water that we receive from Jesus which flows from us by believing in Jesus. Amen.

Reading: John 7 focus: vs. 37-39:

> *On **the last and greatest day of the Feast,** Yeshua stood up and cried out loudly, "If anyone is thirsty, let him come to Me and drink. Whoever believes in Me, as the Scripture says, 'out of his innermost being will flow rivers of living water.'*

Attention: In Chapter 4, John introduces us to the truth of Jesus and that He is the source and giver of "living water" (vs. 10). Today, John testifies of Jesus quoting the O.T. (Isaiah 58:11). *Then Adonai will guide you continually, satisfy your soul in drought and strengthen your bones.*

The Holy Spirit through John says, *Whoever believes in Me, as the Scripture says, out of his innermost being will flow rivers of living water*. The "innermost being" is your deepest emotions of your heart. Those that you feel at a gut level. I was just talking about this with The Widows Project leadership last week. We find that we are ministering to those who have lost a spouse and are grieving at this deep level. Notice what Jesus said, "Whoever believes in Me". The names of those who are "truly born again" are written in His book of life, and they are characterized by "river of living water" flowing out of them. What does that look like? You will manifest by spiritually doing good works like Matthew 25:35-46 and Isaiah 58.

Do you hear? Do you see? It has taken me years to see this and understand. Jesus wants our whole heart, and He has our whole heart when we are loving Him and loving others.

Action: I will teach, mentor and disciple people to follow Jesus daily.

Yielding: leads to finding purpose! Purpose gives you something to live and die for.

Engage: When you are fully engaged with Jesus and His Word, "living water" will flow.

Relationship: It's all about "abiding" in Jesus.

Prayer: Father, I pray that people around us would get splashed upon as we minister the gospel and minister to their needs. Let the "rivers of living water" flow through me! Amen!

Memory verse: John 7:37b-38

> *If anyone is thirsty, let him come to Me and drink.*

> *Whoever believes in Me, as the Scripture says, 'out of his innermost being will flow rivers of living water.'*

Music video: Vinesong - Let Your Living Water Flow,

Thank You Lord, My Life is in Your Hands - Brooklyn Tabernacle Choir

Remember: Abide in Jesus today.

JOHN 8

Prayer: Open our eyes, Lord, to see the truths that You have spoken to us through the Scriptures. Make us aware, that if we are not Yours, we are not free. If we are not Yours, we are not walking in light. If we are not walking in light, we are lost. Amen.

Reading: John 8 key: vs.31-33

> *Then Yeshua said to the Judeans who had trusted Him, "If you abide in My Word, then you are truly My disciples. You will know the truth, and the truth will set you free!" They answered Him, "We are Abraham's children and have never been slaves to anyone! How can you say, 'You will become free'?"*

Attention: Have you ever been lost in the woods? Back in the mid-70's I was interested in hunting and found a couple buddies to hunt deer and elk with. I remember vividly a weekend hunt with one buddy in the Rattlesnake area in the Cascade mountains, near Yakima. We were driving on a logging road and as we arrived in the area, I gave my buddy an overview of the land and how the logging roads ran so that if he felt lost, he would know which way to head and find a logging road. We agreed on a time to meet back at the truck and went our separate ways.

It is easy in the woods to get disoriented, and your mind can play tricks on you. You want to take note of your surroundings, key geographic features, so that as you walk back out, you recognize a certain tree or bend in a path or a rock feature, which assures you of being on the right path.

Well, my buddy got disoriented and was walking north and not east. He ended up in elk beds and snow that was up to his arm pits. He was scared and it was getting late. He fortunately spotted a couple hunters across a valley and got their attention. When he arrived to them, he let them know he was lost and wondered where he was. The other hunters pulled out a map of the area and showed him where he was. Fortunately, he remembered the logging road number we had parked, and they drove him to the truck. I was

117

concerned because by the time he arrived back at the truck, it was dark. He was a couple hours later than our agreed time. His truck also was locked, so I had no way to get inside to stay warm.

After his rescuers left, my buddy recounted his adventure and said he was going to burn the whole forest down if he needed, he felt that desperate, wet, and cold. As he said that, he reached into his pocket for his matches and discovered they were so wet they would not have started any fire. I think at that point he realized he came close to being stranded overnight, and without fire he might have frozen to death. He said in the future, he was going to tie a rope to his waist and the other end to the bumper of his truck.

If we rework Jesus' statement in vs. 31 backwards, it will say *you are truly My disciples, if you abide in My Word.* The character and actions of a true disciple is our "do".

Most of the men reading this have been married or are married. Would you have gotten to know your wife if you hadn't spent time with her? Why did you spend time with her? I assume it was because you loved her.

If you are not aware, Jesus is called the "bridegroom" for a reason. True disciples are called "brides." I hope you are "abiding" in Jesus because you are falling in love with Him. John develops the action of "abiding" in Jesus and His Word in Chapter 15, and you will learn more about abiding in the coming readings.

Action: Jesus I long to "abide" in You and Your Word. I will make a commitment to make being in Your Word my daily lifestyle!

Yielding: I will give you first place, Jesus. (Colossians 1:18b)

Engage: I will engage in daily lifestyle study of the Bible.

Response: I am Yours, Lord!

Memory Verse: John 8:47

He who belongs to God hears the words of God. The reason you don't hear is because you do not belong to God.

Music video: Gaither Vocal Band – I'm Yours, Lord

Remember: Abide in Jesus today.

JOHN 9

Prayer: Father, we choose You, we choose life. Open our eyes that we may see and have new vision which only You can give. May we not be as the Pharisees who by their question, implicated themselves. In Jesus' name. Amen.

Reading: John 9 key: vs. 35-38

> *Yeshua heard that they had thrown him out. Finding him, He said, "Do you believe in the Son of Man?" The man answered, "Who is He, Sir? Tell me, so that I may believe in Him!" Yeshua said, "You have seen Him—He is the One speaking with you." He said, "Lord, I believe!" And he worshiped Him.*

Attention: About ten years ago I had the Lasik procedure done to my eyes. It is an amazing surgery which reshapes your eyes, correcting your vision. When the doctor explained it, it sounded simple and easy. When you think about a very sharp knife cutting your cornea, it sounds painful. Have you ever scratched your eye or gotten something in your eye? It is certainly uncomfortable and hyper-sensitive.

I recovered from the surgery quickly and new vision was restored almost immediately. Notice that the blind man had been blind since birth. He had never seen what mankind or God's creation looked like. He could only imagine, and here he was face to face with Jesus. We don't know how old the man was, but his parents' response to questioning by the Judean leaders tells us that he was old enough to speak for himself. They wanted no part of the leaders' wrath.

We see that the now-seeing man was so repetitively questioned that he became exasperated. At one point he asked the leaders, "You don't want to become His disciple too, do you?" John says, "They railed against him and said, "You're a disciple of that One, but we're disciples of Moses!" Obviously, when pressed, they declared allegiance to Moses.

After they threw this man out of the synagogue, Jesus "found him." He asked, "Do you believe in the Son of Man?" The man answered, "Who is He, Sir? Tell me, so that I may believe in Him." Yeshua said, "You have seen Him—He is the One speaking with you." He said, "Lord, I believe!" And he worshiped Him.

Do you believe? This is the question everyone must answer for themselves. Do you believe? If you do, declare it (tell somebody) and worship Him!

Action: Lord, I believe and declare my love and obedience for You.

Yield: I will show my love for Jesus by worshiping Him.

Engage: In intentional worship and fellowship!

Relationship: I choose intentional relationship with Jesus and people of faith.

Prayer: Lord, thank You for the example of the blind man and his declaration of faith in You. May our faith and love for You move us to worship You in spirit and truth! In Jesus' name. Amen.

Memory verse: John 9:41

Yeshua said to them, "If you were blind, you would have no sin. But now you say, 'We see.' So your sin remains.

Music: Lauren Talley – Lord, I believe In You; Dallas Holm – I Believe in You

Remember: Abide in Jesus today.

I AM

Prayer: Father, I approach You as a son and ask Your Holy Spirit to teach me today. Open my eyes and heart to receive instruction and insight. I desire to be transformed by the renewing of my mind.

Reading: John 10:7, 9, 11 & 14

> *So Yeshua said again, "Amen, amen I tell you, I am the gate for the sheep. I am the gate! If anyone comes in through Me, he will be saved. He will come and go and find pasture. I am the Good Shepherd. The Good Shepherd lays down His life for the sheep. I am the Good Shepherd. I know My own and My own know Me,*

Attention: In this chapter, Jesus makes several "I Am" statements about Himself: I am the gate, and I am the Good Shepherd.

In former chapters of John, Jesus has claimed, *I—the One speaking to you—I am (4:26)", "I am the bread of life" (6:35, 48, 51)", and "I am the light of the world"* (8:12).

Each statement gives us further knowledge about who Jesus is in relation to God. He is God and is claiming that God is His Father.

Statements like this about Himself adds to their confusion as they know Joseph is His earthly father. They believed that a Messiah was coming. Jesus just didn't fit how they perceived and believed He would come. They expected a King who would set up an earthly kingdom and rule.

The first mention of God's name is found in Exodus 3:13-14 when Moses asks God:

> *Suppose I go to Bnei-Yisrael and say to them, The God of your fathers has sent me to you,' and they ask me, "What is His Name? What should I say to them?" God answered Moses, "I AM WHO I AM" Then He said, "You are to say to Bnei-Yisrael, 'I AM' has sent me to you." Literally, "I AM the One who Is".*

We will see more I AM statements by Jesus through the book of

John. Watch for them as we study together.

It is important to ask yourself each time you see an "I AM" statement, "Do I accept and believe Jesus statement about Himself?" Why? Because it is another piece of Jesus' deity. He is fully God and fully man. He is the first and only man wrapped in deity.

Action: I believe that Jesus is God in the flesh.

Yield: I believe that Jesus is the Good Shepherd, the Bread of Life, the Living Water and the Light of the World!

Engage: As a child and sheep of Jesus, I will follow the Good Shepherd.

Relationship: The relationship is like Psalm 23 says, T*he Lord is my shepher*d.

Memory Verse: Psalm 23

A psalm of David. Adonai is my shepherd, I shall not want. He makes me lie down in green pastures. He leads me beside still waters. He restores my soul. He guides me in paths of righteousness for His Name's sake. Even though I walk through the valley of the shadow of death, I will fear no evil, for You are with me: Your rod and Your staff comfort me. You prepare a table before me in the presence of my enemies. You have anointed my head with oil, my cup overflows. Surely goodness and mercy will follow me all the days of my life, and I will dwell in the House of Adonai forever.

Music: Mark Schultz – I AM

Remember: Abide in Jesus today.

JOHN 11

Prayer: Father, I ask that You strengthen my faith. Help me to walk by faith and not by sight. Help me to keep my eyes focused on You. Help me keep my ears tuned to You only as my single source. In Jesus' name, Amen.

Reading: John 11:21-25

> *Martha said to Yeshua, "Master, if You had been here, my brother wouldn't have died! But I know, even now, that whatever You may ask of God, He will give You." Yeshua said to her, "Your brother will rise again." Martha said to Him, "I know, he will rise again in the resurrection on the last day." Yeshua said to her, "I am the resurrection and the life! Whoever believes in Me, even if he dies, shall live.*

Attention: I love the faith Martha exhibits in this passage. Even though she doesn't understand, she affirms her belief that "whatever You may ask of God, He will give You." Even if she didn't fully understand who Jesus is, she believed He had influence with God. When Jesus asked on her behalf, He got results.

It was recently that I gained additional understanding about the role of the Holy Spirit. We are told in Romans 8:26-27:

> *In the same way, the Ruach helps in our weakness. For we do not know how to pray as we should, but the Ruach Himself intercedes for us with groans too deep for words. And He who searches the hearts knows the mind of the Ruach, because He intercedes for the kedoshim (saints, holy ones) according to the will of God.*

Do you realize that the Holy Spirit intercedes on your behalf? Who better to have praying for you than the Holy Spirit? How encouraging to know that we have not only another comforter, teacher, mentor but we also have an advocate who intercedes for us ***according to the will of God***.

The greatest I Am statement Jesus ever made is, ***I Am the resurrection and the Life!*** *Whoever believes in Me, even if he dies,* *shall live. And whoever lives and believes in Me shall never die.*

I ask you the same question Jesus asked after making this statement, ***do you believe this?***

Action: I believe You (Jesus) are the resurrection and the Life!

Yielded: I submit my life to You, Jesus.

Engage: I engage when I am obedient and exercise "active, intentional faith."

Relationship: I love You,Jesus, with my whole heart, mind and soul.

Memory verse: John 11:25

> *Yeshua said to her, "I am the resurrection and the life! Whoever believes in Me, even if he dies, shall live.*

Music: The Hymn Project – My Hope is Built on Nothing Less

Remember: Abide in Jesus today.

JOHN 12

Prayer: Father, I pray that everyone reading today's reading in John, will see Jesus as the Way, the Truth, and the Life! To choose to follow Jesus is to choose life! Choosing Jesus is the greatest choice a person can make in their life! Give them the courage and power to say, "I will follow Jesus!" Amen.

Reading: John 12 focus: 23-28

> *Yeshua answers them, saying, "The hour has come for the Son of Man to be glorified! Amen, amen I tell you, unless a grain of wheat falls to the earth and dies, it remains alone. But if it dies, it produces much fruit. He who loves his life will lose it, and the one who hates his life in this world will keep it forever. If any man serves Me, he must follow Me; and where I am, there also will My servant be. If anyone serves Me, the Father will honor him.*
>
> *"Now My soul is troubled. And what shall I say? 'Father, save Me from this hour'? But it was for this reason I came to this hour. Father, glorify Your name!"*
>
> *Then a voice came out of heaven, "I have glorified it, and again I will glorify it!"*

Attention: Have you ever had to make a tough decision. One which required you to make a choice that you would have to live with the rest of your life? Or, one which will affect your life or another's for eternity? If you are my age, you may have made several life choices. Jesus was facing what He came for, to die for the sins of the world.

Deitrich Bonhoeffer: "When Christ calls a man, he **bids** him **come and die.**"

If you have never heard of Deitrich Bonhoeffer, I would encourage you to get a copy of Eric Metaxas' book, ***7 Men – And The Secret of Their Greatness***. Bonhoeffer was a German pastor who, "because of his Christian faith, stood up for Germany's Jews and got involved in the plot to assassinate Adolf Hitler." Bonhoeffer was captured, imprisoned and hung three weeks before the war ended. He paid with his life.

Might Jesus require the same of you or I? We may never be required to die for our faith, but we are all asked to choose who we will serve. Glorify Jesus today by committing your life anew to Him who died for you. Choose Life!

Action: I will "choose life" today and will follow Jesus.

Yielded: A yielded life is a committed life!

Engaged: An engaged life find its "do".

Relationship: Paul says, *"For to me, to lie is Messiah and to die is gain."* Philippians 1:21

Prayer: Father I pray Deuteronomy 30:19-20 over everyone reading this today.

> *I call the heavens and the earth to witness about you today, that I have set before you life and death, the blessing and the curse. Therefore choose life so that you and your descendants may live, by loving Adonai your God, listening to His voice, and clinging to Him. For He is your life and the length of your days, that you may dwell on the land that Adonai swore to your fathers—to Abraham, to Isaac and to Jacob—to give them.*

May they "choose life" today in Jesus' name, Amen!

Memory Scripture: John 12:44-45

> *Yeshua cried out, "Whoever puts trust in Me believes not in Me but in the One who sent Me! And whoever beholds Me beholds the One who sent Me.*

Music: Keith Green - I Pledge My Head to Heaven;

Ray Boltz - I Pledge Allegiance To The Lamb:

Remember: Abide in Jesus today.

JOHN 13

Prayer: Father, may I want You more than the blessing. May I understand, blessings come from obedience. How can I expect blessing when I am not living my life for You? May I resolve the conflict of choosing Your way or the world's way. I choose life and I choose blessing! In Jesus' name, amen.

Reading: John 13 Focus: vs 13

If *you know these things, you are blessed* **if** *you* ***do them!***

Attention: Jesus made several conditional statements and the Holy Spirit, through men who wrote the Scriptures, made conditional statements. Here is an example of a well-known, of quoted Scripture that demonstrates a "conditional statement." It is found in 2 Chronicles 7:13-14.

If I shut up heaven that there is no rain, or if I command the locust to devour the land, or if I send pestilence among My people, when My people, over whom My Name is called, humble themselves and pray and seek My face and turn from their evil ways, then I will hear from heaven and will forgive their sin and will heal their land.

John quotes Jesus with just the same kind of conditions, *"**If** you know these things, **you are blessed if you do them!**"* It is our "do" that activates the blessing. It is our obedience. It is our actions. It is our acts of service. They each are "do's".

Action: I want to be blessed so; I will perform an act of service today.

Yield: By our "do" we yield our lives to Jesus.

Engage: Doing is engaging in Jesus lifestyle.

Repurpose: I am "purposed" when I am "repurposed" by Jesus.

Prayer: Father, I pray for those You have entrusted to me to disciple. May they see and understand the system of daily lifestyle in Your Word. May we be desperate for You. Desperate for a touch from You. Desperate to know You. Desperate for our children to know

You. Keep us close to You. I pray in Jesus' name. Amen.

Memory verse: John 13:34-35

> *I give you a new commandment, that you love one another. Just as I have loved you, so also you must love one another. By this all will know that you are My disciples, if you have love for one another.*

Music: Hillsong: I Surrender

Remember: Abide in Jesus today.

JOHN 14

Prayer: Father, I pray for fresh eyes and an open heart to see Your Word today. I am ready for instruction. My mind is prepared to receive mentoring from the Holy Spirit. In Jesus' name. Amen.

Reading: John 14 Key: vs. 1-4

> *Do not let your heart be troubled. Trust in God; trust also in Me. In My Father's house there are many dwelling places. If it were not so, would I have told you that I am going to prepare a place for you? If I go and prepare a place for you, I will come again and take you to Myself, so that where I am you may also be. And you know the way to where I am going.*

Attention: I have heard it said of men that we have a recessive gene when it comes to asking for directions. Today we have GPS devices on our phones and while they become more accurate, they are not foolproof. I have experienced ending up somewhere else and calling the party I am trying to find.

After Jesus makes some amazing claims in the opening verses of Chapter 14, Thomas chimes up and says, *"we don't know where You are going. How can we know the way?"*

Yeshua (Jesus) said to him, *"I am the way, the truth, and the life!"* The directions seem clear to me! Jesus is the way to God, our Father.

I heard a pastor say recently, that people argue the claim that Jesus is the only way. His argument was, if you were given a physical address and were given directions and chose to go a different way, would you end up where you wanted to go? Many of us in life have gotten diverted and tried to take other avenues to find Jesus. I ask you, how is that working for you? Have you lived long enough to have discovered that you have not found who you are looking for by taking different paths? You can course correct at any time by repenting and confessing your sin.

I encourage you to make this choice, this decision today, to follow Jesus. He truly is the only way!

Action: I choose to confess Jesus is the only way!

Yielded: A yielded life is a surrendered life!

Engage: I will commit to a daily lifestyle plan of time with God in His Word with journaling.

Relationship: My life is so much better when it is lived in harmony with God!

Prayer: Father, I repent of trying to live my life on my own. Restore unto me the joy of my salvation. I hunger and thirst for You. Conform me to Your image and transform my mind by renewing it. Give me a new heart that yearns for You. In Jesus' (Yeshua's) name. Amen.

Memory verse: John 14:15-17 or vs. 26

> *If you love Me, you will keep My commandments. I will ask the Father, and He will give you another Helper so He may be with you forever—the Spirit of truth, whom the world cannot receive, because it does not behold Him or know Him. You know Him, because He abides with you and will be in you.*
>
> *But the Helper, the Ruach ha-Kodesh whom the Father will send in My name, will teach you everything and remind you of everything that I said to you.*

Music: Pat Barrett - The Way

Remember: Abide in Jesus today.

ABIDE WITH ME

Prayer: Father, good morning! It is good to see Your face first thing when I awake. I love spending the first of my day with You. Help me to capture and communicate what relationship with You looks and feels like. Thank You for another day with You. Amen.

Reading: John 15

> *¹ I am the true vine, and My Father is the gardener. ² Every branch in Me that does not bear fruit, He takes away; and every branch that bears fruit, He trims so that it may bear more fruit. ³ You are already clean because of the word I have spoken to you. ⁴ Abide in Me, and I will abide in you. The branch cannot itself produce fruit, unless it abides on the vine. Likewise, you cannot produce fruit unless you abide in Me.*

> *⁵ "I am the vine; you are the branches. The one who abides in Me, and I in him, bears much fruit; for apart from Me, you can do nothing. ⁶ If anyone does not abide in Me, he is thrown away like a branch and is dried up. Such branches are picked up and thrown into the fire and burned.*

> *⁷ "If you abide in Me and My words abide in you, ask whatever you wish, and it shall be done for you. ⁸ In this My Father is glorified, that you bear much fruit and so prove to be My disciples."*

> *⁹ "Just as the Father has loved Me, I also have loved you. Abide in My love! ¹⁰ If you keep My commandments, you will abide in My love, just as I have kept My Father's commandments and abide in His love. ¹¹ These things I have spoken to you so that My joy may be in you, and your joy may be full.*

> *¹² "This is My commandment, that you love one another just as I have loved you. ¹³ No one has greater love than this: that he lay down his life for his friends. ¹⁴ You are My friends if you do what I command you.*

¹⁵ *"I am no longer calling you servants, for the servant does not know what his master is doing. Now I have called you friends, because everything I have heard from My Father I have made known to you.*

¹⁶ *"You did not choose Me, but I chose you. I selected you so that you would go and produce fruit, and your fruit would remain. Then the Father will give you whatever you ask in My name.*
¹⁷ *"These things I command you,*
so that you may love one another."

¹⁸ *If the world hates you, know that it has hated Me before you. ¹⁹ If you were out of the world, the world would love you as its own. But you are not of the world, since I have chosen you out of the world; therefore the world hates you.*

²⁰ *"Remember the word I spoke to you: 'A servant is not greater than his master.' If they persecuted Me, they will persecute you also. If they kept My Word, they will keep yours also. ²¹ "But all these things they will do to you for the sake of My name, because they do not know the One who sent Me. ²² If I had not come and spoken to them, they would have no sin. But now they have no excuse for their sin.*

²³ *"He who hates Me also hates My Father. ²⁴ If I had not done works among them that no one else did, they would have no sin. But now they have seen and have hated both Me and My Father. ²⁵ So is fulfilled the word written in their Scripture, 'They hated Me for no reason.' ²⁶ "When the Helper comes—whom I will send to you from the Father, the Spirit of truth who goes out from the Father— He will testify about Me. ²⁷ And you also testify, because you have been with Me from the beginning."*

Focus: Consider circling or highlighting every 'abide' in this chapter. How many did you find? Do you think there was a purpose to the repetition of the word 'abide'?

Attention: Have you ever observed or experienced a toddler who is at complete and total comfort with his father? Climbing up on his lap and sitting in the security of daddy's protective presence. Surveying the world within proximity to his purview. All is well.

The picture I get from John's writing is one like this toddler who is completely at comfort in his father's presence. This is the best description I can provide of the concept of 'abiding' in Jesus. We were told in Chapter 14 that Jesus would send 'another comforter', which tells me that Jesus too is a comforter. Can we who are His ever have too much comfort? Can we ever have too much assurance of His comfort and presence?

Enjoy intentional 'abiding in Jesus', today!

Action: I will abide in Jesus today!

Yielded: I surrender to abiding in Jesus 24/7.

Engaged: I choose to be in His presence at all times.

Relationship: I feel the most comfort when I am abiding in Jesus.

Prayer: Jesus, it is pretty simple, isn't it? When I abide in You, You abide in Me. When I abide in Your Word, Your Word abides in me. When I am attached to You I feel the most comfort! Keep me close! In Jesus' name, Amen.

Memory Verse: John 15:12

> *This is My commandment, that you love one another just as I have loved you.*

Music: Matt Maher - Abide with Me

Remember: Abide in Jesus today.

JOHN 16

Prayer: Father, in these chaotic days I pray for peace that is unlike anything the world comprehends. I pray You will keep in perfect peace those whose minds are fixed on You. Hold our hands Lord, in this darkened world. Amen.

Reading: John 16 Key: vs. 33

> *These things I have spoken to you, so that in Me you may have shalom. In the world you will have trouble, but take heart! I have overcome the world!*

Attention: In the early part of this chapter, Jesus shares with us six characteristics of or roles of the Holy Spirit, whom Jesus calls "the Helper".

- He will convict the world about sin
- He will convict the world concerning righteousness (because Jesus is going to the Father)
- He will convict the world concerning judgement (satan has been judged)
- He will guide us into all the truth
- He will declare to you the things that are to come
- He will glorify Me (Jesus)

Isn't it glorious that God the Father, Jesus, and the Holy Spirit work in total oneness and cooperation? They are each distinct, yet One. Remember, God sent Jesus, and Jesus sent the Holy Spirit after His ascension into heaven on the day of Pentecost (or 50 days after His resurrection).

While Jesus acknowledges the apostle's grief over the things He was telling them, He tells them that unless He leaves, the Holy Spirit will not come. His entire message culminates in vs. 33, *"These things I have spoken to you, so that in Me you may have shalom. In the world you will have trouble, but take heart! I have overcome the world."*

I pray that you will experience an extra measure of "shalom" (peace) because you have read these words and have been reminded that the Holy Spirit is with you, and in you, and upon you as you go throughout your day. This is a promise to those who are in Jesus.

Action: I will walk in confident assurance of the Holy Spirit's presence with me today. I acknowledge today the Holy Spirit guiding me into all truth!

Yielding: Holy Spirit transform my life through Your Word.

Engage: I will actively keep my mind focused on Jesus today, and actively reduce or eliminate messages from the world that bring a different message or narrative to you.

Reliance: Total trust in Jesus and the Holy Spirit to give you peace.

Prayer: Jesus, thank You for sending the Holy Spirit who leads me and guides me as I read the Bible. I acknowledge the truth of Your Word as a light unto my path. Please order my steps according to Your Word! In Jesus' name. Amen.

Memory Verse: John 16:23-24

> *In that day, you will ask Me nothing. Amen, amen I tell you, whatever you ask the Father in My name, He will give you. Up to now, you have not asked for anything in My name. Ask and you will receive, so that your joy may be full.*

Music: Maranatha- Heavenly Father I Appreciate You; Kari Jobe - Holy Spirit You are Welcome Here

Remember: Abide in Jesus today.

JOHN 17

Prayer: Father, I thank You for another day and more time to walk in step with You. I come ready this morning to be taught and mentored by Your Holy Spirit. I come with a ready spirit and mind. Open my eyes and reveal to me truth from Your Word. In Jesus' name. Amen.

Reading: John 17 Key: 20-26

> *20 "I pray not on behalf of these only, but also for those who believe in Me through their message, 21 that they all may be one. Just as You, Father, are in Me and I am in You, so also may they be one in Us, so the world may believe that You sent Me. 22 The glory that You have given to Me I have given to them, that they may be one just as We are one— 23 I in them and You in Me—that they may be perfected in unity, so that the world may know that You sent Me and loved them as You loved Me.*
>
> *24 "Father, I also want those You have given Me to be with Me where I am, so that they may see My glory—the glory You gave Me, for You loved Me before the foundation of the world. 25 Righteous Father, the world did not know You, but I knew You; and these knew that You sent Me. 26 I made your Name known to them, and will continue to make it known, so that the love with which You loved Me may be in them, and I in them."*

Attention: This chapter has become known as the "High Priestly Prayer." I invite you to pay special attention to the various things Jesus asks on the behalf of His disciples.

I will list several of them momentarily, but I want to draw your attention to an aspect of praying that I didn't pay as much attention to until 2020. Do you realize that your prayers, like those of Jesus, speak forward into future generations? God established covenants with the Hebrew nation, Israel, in the Old Testament. His covenants span generations.

Jesus, as God and like God, spoke a new covenant in the

New Testament. His prayers and our prayers extend to generation after generation. When you are praying for your children, realize that your DNA extends for generations. Realize, that God told Abraham that his "seed" would number "*like the stars*" (Gen. 15:5).

Would your awareness influence the way you pray?

Here is a quick list of things Jesus prayed for you:

- Keep us from the "evil one." vs. 15
- Request to make us "holy in the truth" vs 18
- Those who hear the message through followers of Jesus vs. 20
- Followers of Jesus will be one with God, Jesus, and Holy Spirit (Us) vs. 21
- Oneness of followers vs. 22-3
- Followers/Disciples to "*be with Me*" in Heaven vs. 24
- His love would be in us vs. 26

How wonderful to know that Jesus prayed for me before I was even formed in my mother's womb!

Action: I will pray for my children and my children's children for they are my heritage.

Yielding: My prayers influence generations of my family.

Engage: Prayer is an action. Prayer is active. Prayer activates God.

Relationship: Prayer is a relational activity to God and with the Holy Spirit on behalf of God, Jesus, the Holy Spirit and others.

Memory verse: John 17:3

> *And this is eternal life, that they may know You, the only true God, and Yeshua the Messiah, the One You sent.*

Music: Kari Jobe & Cody Carnes - The Blessing

Remember: Abide in Jesus today.

JOHN 18

Prayer: Father thank You for the awareness that You are for us! That even in our sleep, You are working in us and on our behalf. You love us so much! Jesus loves us so much that He spread His hands wide, saying, "I love you this much." Thank You for "so loving" us that You gave Yourself! Amen.

Reading: John 18 Key: vs. 33-37

> *33 So Pilate went back into the Praetorium, called for Yeshua, and asked Him, "Are you the King of the Jews?"*
>
> *34 "Are you saying this on your own," Yeshua answered, "or did others tell you about Me?"*
>
> *35 Pilate answered, "I'm not a Jew, am I? Your own nation and ruling kohanim handed You over to me! What have You done?"*
>
> *36 Yeshua answered, "My kingdom is not of this world. If My kingdom were of this world, then My servants would be fighting so that I wouldn't be handed over to the Judean leaders. But as it is, My kingdom is not from here."*
>
> *37 So Pilate said to Him, "Are you a king, then?"*
>
> *Yeshua answered, "You say that I am a king. For this reason I was born, and for this reason I came into the world, so that I might testify to the truth. Everyone who is of the truth hears My voice."*

Attention: In Jesus' dialogue with Pilate, He establishes with Pilate that He is not a threat to his kingdom, but Pilate ascertains from the conversation that Jesus is a King. He even asks Him point blank, *"Are you a King then?"* Jesus answers in the affirmative, *"For this reason I was born, and for this reason I came into the world, so that I might testify to the truth."* Just as He called each disciple with the invitation "Follow Me" and asked Peter, "Who do you say I Am?", we must answer "Is Jesus King of my life?" He established His Kingdom on earth as it is in heaven. He must have subjects to fill His

Kingdom and those whose names are written in the Book of Life to fill heaven. That where He is, we might be also.

Do you consider Him the King of your life? Does He sit on the throne of your heart? How differently would you read Scripture and live your life if He was on the throne?

Action: Lord, I surrender my heart and ask You to take up residence as my King!

Yield: Surrender is an action done unto a King!

Engage: In His Kingdom work. Ask the Holy Spirit to show you your purpose.

Relinquish: Give Him control of your life and ask Him to order your steps.

Prayer: King Jesus, take control of my life, my desires, my hopes and dreams. Reveal to me Your purposes for my life! I am Yours, Lord, everything I am and everything I need and everything I want. I am Yours Lord! Amen.

Memory verse: John 18:37

So Pilate said to Him, "Are you a king, then?"

Yeshua answered, "You say that I am a king. For this reason I was born, and for this reason I came into the world, so that I might testify to the truth. Everyone who is of the truth hears My voice."

Music video: Mark Shultz- I AM; S.M. Lockridge -That's My King

Remember: Abide in Jesus today.

JOHN 19

Prayer: Father thank You for the honor of serving You. Thank You for revealing more of Yourself every day. Thank You that even after years of study You open my eyes to new revelation. Your Word is fresh and new every day, like the manna you provided the Hebrew children. Thank You for fresh spiritual and physical food. In Jesus' name. Amen.

Reading: John 19 key vs. 41-42

> *⁴¹ Now in the place where He was executed, there was a garden. In the garden was a new tomb where no one had yet been buried. ⁴² Because it was the Jewish Day of Preparation and the tomb was nearby, they laid Yeshua there.*

Attention: Something popped off the pages of Chapter 19 today. Have you ever been driving along the road, or a highway, and you notice something you haven't noticed before? I recall an experience like that about five years ago. I had a regular backroad route to work and suddenly I noticed an empty piece of property with a fantastic view of the Cascade Mountain range and a partial view of the Sound. I mentally tagged the location and have visited the property and prayed over it many times.

Today when I was reading "there was a garden", I passed and took notice of it in a new way. Did you notice the garden, or did you read right past it? I knew instantly that I had noticed "there was a garden" in a previous, recent reading. Take a look back at 18:1, "there was a garden". Jesus entered a garden prior to his arrest, and He entered a garden at His death burial. We are told it was a "new tomb" He was placed in.

Where does life begin? In a garden. Where did life begin? In the garden of Eden (Gen. 2:7-10a).

> *⁷ Then Adonai Elohim formed the man out of the dust from the ground and He breathed into his nostrils a breath of life—so the man became a living being. ⁸ Then Adonai Elohim planted a garden in Eden in the east, and there He put the man whom He had formed. ⁹ Then Adonai Elohim caused to*

sprout from the ground every tree that was desirable to look at and good for food.

Now the Tree of Life was in the middle of the garden, and also the Tree of Knowledge of Good and Evil. ¹⁰ A river flowed out of Eden to water the garden.

Life began in a garden, the garden of Eden, and "New Life" arose in a garden. I hope that you will notice "there was a garden" the next time you read this passage because it is where your life began both physically and spiritually.

Bonus: We recently read John 15. Look at vs. 1. Who does Jesus declare is the "gardener"?

Action: I acknowledge God as the gardener of my life and Jesus as the "vine".

Yielded: I surrender ownership of my life to Jesus.

Engage: Plant yourself into a daily lifestyle of time in the Word.

Rest: Receive the rest that Jesus gives us every week. He rested too!

Prayer: Jesus how majestic is your name in all the earth! Amen.

Memory verse: John 19:11

¹¹ Yeshua answered, "You would have no authority over Me if it hadn't been given to you from above. For this reason, the one who handed Me over to you has the greater sin."

Music video: Alan Jackson - In the Garden

Remember: Abide in Jesus today.

JOHN 20

IT WAS EARLY IN THE MORNING

Prayer: Good morning, Father. I love being up with You in the early morning and conversing. I pray that everyone reading this journal will relate with the content and see You in a new and fresh way. May these words trigger additional Holy Spirit fueled thoughts about Jesus and the 40 days after His resurrection. Thank You for revealing Yourself to us through John's witness. In Jesus' name. Amen.

Reading: John 20 key: vs. 1-2

> *Early in the morning on the first day of the week, while it is still dark, Miriam from Magdala comes to the tomb. She sees that the stone had been rolled away from the tomb. So she comes running to Simon Peter and the other disciple, the one Yeshua loved. She tells them, "They've taken the Master out of the tomb, and we don't know where they've put Him!"*

Attention: I never used to be an early morning person. I would prefer to stay up late and sleep in over beating the sunrise. I have discovered, however, the benefits of starting my day in the Word. It prepares me for the day ahead. It gives me the right mindset and attitude. It renews my spirit. It directs my focus vertically and sets the world right horizontally.

Early morning is the one part of my day that I can control as it is usually free from distraction. Invariably, my experience is when I don't get my time with God accomplished in the early morning, life comes and steals the ability to get back to God. I found I had to be "very intentional" early on, until my appointment with God became a lifestyle. You will experience the same if you persevere and discipline yourself.

Miriam couldn't wait. Her anxiety had to be fulfilled. Did Jesus do what He claimed He would do. It was the third day. She had to know. John tells us, *"Early in the morning.... while it was still dark, Miriam...comes to the tomb."* She sees that the *"stone had been rolled away from the tomb"* and her first thoughts are, *"They've taken the Master out of the tomb, and we don't know where they've put Him!"* Anxiety overwhelms Miriam.

Do we not do the same? Do we not fear the unknown? Yet, through the witness of John, Jesus wants us to know the truth. Therefore, John ends this chapter with these words, *"these things have been written so that you may believe that Yeshua is Ben-Elohim, and that by believing you may have life in His name."*

I hope that you find those words comforting. Miriam's anxiety was comforted when she discovered Jesus' body had not been stolen as she feared, but He indeed resurrected and proved it to her. Jesus' appearances over the next 40 days prior to His ascension are documented by scores of eyewitnesses (1 Corinthians 15:1-8).

Rejoice with me today. Jesus is alive, and He lives in you and me.

Action: Jesus, I purpose to meet with You in the early morning just like Miriam.

Yield: Lord, help my faith to grow in You.

Engage: Help me to establish a daily lifestyle of time with You, Jesus, in the early morning!

Restore: Unto me the joy of my salvation.

Memory verse: 2 Timothy 1:12b

> *...for I know in whom I have trusted and I am convinced He is able to safeguard what I have entrusted to Him until that Day.*

Music Video: Hope Darst - Peace Be Still; Wintley Phipps - It is Well with my Soul

Remember: Abide in Jesus today.

JOHN 21

Prayer: Father, You continue to reinforce a morning meeting with You. Even in Your Word, You mention the time of day as having significance. You give order to creation with day and night and stars that have greater or lesser light. You even tell us that "today is the day You have made, let us rejoice in it." Thank You for the "daily bread" You provide for us. In Jesus' name above all names. Amen.

Reading: John 21 Key-vs. 9-12a

> *⁹ So when they got out onto the land, they saw a charcoal fire with fish placed on it, and bread. ¹⁰ Yeshua said to them, "Bring some of the fish you've just caught." ¹¹ Simon Peter went aboard and hauled the net to shore. There were 153 fish, many of them big; but the net was not broken. ¹² Yeshua said to them, "Come, have breakfast." None of the disciples dared ask Him, "Who are You?"—knowing it was the Lord.*

Attention: Have you ever known a fisherman that didn't get up and out to the water by the first light of the day? In fact, have you noticed there seems to be something magical about opening day? The anticipation for a true sport fisherman is palpable. Probably much like a child's anticipation of their birthday or Christmas. They have stood on the shores during the winter and envisioned good weather and excellent results.

However, for the disciples, arising early was probably more a requirement of the trade. The fish feed in the morning and evening. Fishermen know that there are times of the day which increase their odds of success, and getting to the prime spots first are vitally important. This is their livelihood, and their families depend on them.

The same skills and character required to become a disciple of Jesus arise from becoming a good fisherman. If you are a fisherman, do you get up early to get to your fishing hole first? Are you a patient fisherman? Do you persevere? Are you easily discouraged if you don't catch anything? Do you study the various techniques and tools of the trade?

There is much that we can learn from the fishermen in the Bible. There is more we can learn from the Bible about Jesus and His purpose in making breakfast for the fishermen, His disciples. Think upon these things as you eat breakfast this morning!

Action: I purpose to give You the first portion of my day in reading the Scriptures.

Yield: I yield the first time of my awakened day to You.

Engage: I will be fully involved in time with You, Jesus.

Restored: When I begin with You, Jesus, I am renewed and restored!

Prayer: Jesus, I enjoy my time with You. I desire to seek You early in the morning as our time sets the energy of my day on the right track. Praise You Jesus. Amen.

Memory Verse: Psalm 103:1-5

> *Of David.*
> *Bless Adonai, O my soul,*
> *and all that is within me, bless His holy Name.*
> *² Bless Adonai, O my soul,*
> *and forget not all His benefits:*
> *³ He forgives all your iniquity.*
> *He heals all your diseases.*
> *⁴ He redeems your life from the Pit.*
> *He crowns you with lovingkindness and compassions.*
> *⁵ He satisfies your years with good things,*
> *so that your youth is renewed like an eagle.*

Music Video: John Fischer - All Day Song

Remember: Abide in Jesus today.

STRATEGIC SCRIPTURES FOR THEOLOGICAL FORMATION AND MEMORIZATION

Do I have each of the Scriptures which are contained in this list memorized? No. However, it is from these Scriptures that I have based my concept and character of God, Christ, and the Holy Spirit. From Scripture I have formed a biblical understanding about sin, salvation, grace, faith, law, creation, life, prayer and the Bible. I stand on the authority of the Scriptures as God's words and declarations. Rather than allow the society of the world to tell me what the Bible says, I study diligently so that I can refute the lies of the enemy. I encourage you to do the same. Allow the Word, through the Holy Spirit, to declare to you and the world, thus says the Lord!

Committing these Scriptures to memory will give you command, at a moment's notice, and an answer for the hope that lies within you. Become a Berean (Acts 17:11) in your understanding and command in the Word. Notice that the Bereans were disciplined, studying the Word "each day to see whether these things were true." They were not studying to refute the apostles' teaching. They were studying to confirm they were being taught the truth.

I charge you like Paul commissioned young Timothy,

"In the presence of God and Messiah Yeshua, who is about to judge the living and the dead at His appearing and His Kingdom—proclaim the Word! Be ready when it is convenient or inconvenient. Confront, rebuke, encourage— with complete patience and instruction" (2 Timothy 4:1-2).

ADONAI (GOD)

Genesis 1:1-2: *In the beginning God created the heavens and the earth. Now the earth was chaos and waste, darkness was on the surface of the deep, and the Ruach Elohim (Holy Spirit) was hovering upon the surface of the water.*

Exodus 3:13-15: *But Moses said to God, "Suppose I go to Bnei-Yisrael and say to them, 'The God of your fathers has sent me to you,' and they ask me, 'What is His Name?' What should I say to them?"*

God answered Moses, "I AM WHO I AM. " Then He said, "You are to say to Bnei-Yisrael, 'I AM' has sent me to you."

God also said to Moses: "You are to say to Bnei-Yisrael, Adonai, the God of your fathers, the God of Abraham, Isaac, and Jacob, has sent me to you. This is My Name forever, and the Name by which I should be remembered from generation to generation.

Matthew 22:36-40: *Teacher, which is the greatest commandment in the Torah?"*

And He said to him, "'You shall love Adonai your God with all your heart, and with all your soul, and with all your mind.'

This is the first and greatest commandment.

And the second is like it, 'You shall love your neighbor as yourself.'

The entire Torah and the Prophets hang on these two commandments."

YESHUA (JESUS)

Romans 1:3-4: Concerning His Son, He came into being from the seed of David according to the flesh.

He was appointed *Ben-Elohim* in power according to the *Ruach* of holiness, by the resurrection from the dead. He is Messiah *Yeshua* our Lord.

1 Corinthians 15:3-8, 19-21: For I also passed on to you first of all what I also received— that Messiah died for our sins according to the Scriptures,

that He was buried, that He was raised on the third day according to the Scriptures,

and that He appeared to Kefa, then to the Twelve.

Then He appeared to over five hundred brothers and sisters at one time— most of them are still alive, though some have died.

Then He appeared to Jacob, then to all the emissaries,

and last of all, as to one untimely born, He also appeared to me.

If we have hoped in Messiah in this life alone, we are to be pitied more than all people.

But now Messiah has been raised from the dead, the firstfruits of those who have fallen asleep.

For since death came through a man, the resurrection of the dead also has come through a Man.

RUACH ELOHIM (HOLY SPIRIT)

John 14:25-27: These things I have spoken to you while dwelling with you.

But the Helper, the *Ruach ha-Kodesh* whom the Father will send in My name, will teach you everything and remind you of everything that I said to you.

"*Shalom* I leave you, My *shalom* I give to you; but not as the world gives! Do not let your heart be troubled or afraid.

Galatians 5:22-25: But the fruit of the *Ruach* is love, joy, peace, patience, kindness, goodness, faithfulness,

gentleness, and self-control—against such things there is no law.

Now those who belong to Messiah have crucified the flesh with its passions and desires.

If we live by the *Ruach*, let us also walk by the *Ruach*.

SIN:

Romans 3:23: But now God's righteousness apart from the *Torah* has been revealed, to which the *Torah* and the Prophets bear witness—namely, the righteousness of God through putting trust in Messiah *Yeshua*, to all who keep on trusting. For there is no distinction,

for all have sinned and fall short of the glory of God.

Romans 6:20-23: For when you were slaves of sin, you were free with regard to righteousness.

So then, what outcome did you have that you are now ashamed of? For the end of those things is death.

But now, having been set free from sin and having become

enslaved to God, you have your fruit resulting in holiness. And the outcome is eternal life.

For sin's payment is death, but God's gracious gift is eternal life in Messiah *Yeshua* our Lord.

James 4:17: Therefore whoever knows the right thing to do and does not do it—for him it is sin.

SALVATION:

Acts 4:12: There is salvation in no one else, for there is no other name under heaven given to mankind by which we must be saved!"

John 3:5-7: *Yeshua* answered, "Amen, *amen* I tell you, unless one is born of water and spirit, he cannot enter the kingdom of God.

What is born of the flesh is flesh, and what is born of the Spirit is spirit."

Do not be surprised that I said to you, 'You all must be born from above.'

Romans 10:12-13: For there is no distinction between Jew and Greek, for the same Lord is Lord of all—richly generous to all who call on Him.

For "Everyone who calls upon the name of *Adonai* shall be saved."

GRACE:

Ephesians 2:8-10: For by grace you have been saved through faith. And this is not from yourselves—it is the gift of God.

It is not based on deeds, so that no one may boast.

For we are His workmanship—created in Messiah *Yeshua* for good deeds, which God prepared beforehand so we might walk in them.

FAITH:

Romans 1:17: In it the righteousness of God is revealed, from trust to trust. As it is written, "But the righteous shall live by *Emunah (faith)*."

James 2:26: For just as the body without the spirit is dead, so also faith without works is dead.

BIBLE:

2 Timothy 3:14-17: You, however, continue in what you have learned and what you have become convinced of. For you know from whom you have learned,

and that from childhood you have known the sacred writings that are able to make you wise, leading to salvation through trusting in Messiah *Yeshua.*

All Scripture is inspired by God and useful for teaching, for reproof, for restoration, and for training in righteousness,

so that the person belonging to God may be capable, fully equipped for every good deed.

Hebrews 4:12: For the Word of God is living and active and sharper than any two-edged sword—piercing right through to a separation of soul and spirit, joints and marrow, and able to judge the thoughts and intentions of the heart.

Psalm 119:11 & 105: I have treasured Your Word in my heart, so I might not sin against You. Your Word is a lamp to my feet and a light to my path.

LIFE:

Matthew 7:12: So in all things, do to others what you would want them to do to you—for this is the *Torah* and the Prophets.

Proverbs 3:5-6: Trust in *Adonai* with all your heart, lean not on your own understanding.

In all your ways acknowledge Him, and He will make your paths straight.

CREATION:

Genesis 1:26-27: Then God said, "Let Us make man in Our image, after Our likeness! Let them rule over the fish of the sea, over the flying creatures of the sky, over the livestock, over the whole earth, and over every crawling creature that crawls on the land."

God created humankind in His image, in the image of God He created him, male and female He created them.

Genesis 2:7,21-27: Then *Adonai Elohim* formed the man out of the dust from the ground and He breathed into his nostrils a breath of life—so the man became a living being.

Adonai Elohim caused a deep sleep to fall on the man and he slept; and He took one of his ribs and closed up the flesh in its place.

Adonai Elohim built the rib, which He had taken from the man, into a woman. Then He brought her to the man.

Then the man said, "This one, at last, is bone of my bones and flesh from my flesh. This one is called woman, for from man was taken this one."

This is why a man leaves his father and his mother and clings to his wife; and they become one flesh.

LAW:

Exodus 20:1-17: Then God spoke all these words saying,

"I am *Adonai* your God, who brought you out of the land of Egypt, out of the house of bondage.

"You shall have no other gods before Me.

Do not make for yourself a graven image, or any likeness of anything that is in heaven above or on the earth below or in the water under the earth.

Do not bow down to them, do not let anyone make you serve them. For I, *Adonai* your God, am a jealous God, bringing the iniquity of the fathers upon the children to the third and fourth generations of those who hate Me,

but showing lovingkindness to the thousands of generations of those who love Me and keep My *mitzvot*.

"You must not take the Name of *Adonai* your God in vain, for *Adonai* will not hold him guiltless that takes His Name in vain.

"Remember Yom Shabbat, to keep it holy.

You are to work six days, and do all your work,

but the seventh day is a *Shabbat* to *Adonai* your God. In it you shall not do any work—not you, nor your son, your daughter, your male servant, your female servant, your cattle, nor the outsider that is within your gates.

For in six days *Adonai* made heaven and earth, the sea, and all that is in them, and rested on the seventh day.

Thus *Adonai* blessed Yom Shabbat, and made it holy.

"Honor your father and your mother, so that your days may be long upon the land which *Adonai* your God is giving you.

"Do not murder.

"Do not commit adultery.

"Do not steal.

"Do not bear false witness against your neighbor.

"Do not covet your neighbor's house, your neighbor's wife, his manservant, his maidservant, his ox, his donkey, or anything that is your neighbor's."

Deuteronomy 10:12-13: So now, O Israel, what does *Adonai* your God require of you, but to fear *Adonai* your God, to walk in all His ways and love Him, and to serve *Adonai* your God with all your heart and with all your soul,

to keep the *mitzvot* of *Adonai* and His statutes that I am commanding you today, for your own good?

Deuteronomy 11:26-28: See, I am setting before you today a blessing and a curse—

the blessing, if you listen to the *mitzvot* of *Adonai* your God that I am commanding you today,

but the curse, if you do not listen to the *mitzvot* of *Adonai* your God, but turn from the way I am commanding you today, to go after other gods you have not known."

Deuteronomy 30:6-11,19-20: Also *Adonai* your God will circumcise your heart and the heart of your descendants— to love *Adonai* your God with all your heart and with all your soul, in order that you may live.

"*Adonai* your God will put all these curses on your enemies and on those who hate you, who persecuted you.

Then you—you will return and listen to the voice of *Adonai* and do all His *mitzvot* that I am commanding you today. Then you—you will return and listen to the voice of *Adonai* and do all His *mitzvot* that I am commanding you today.

Adonai your God will make you prosper in all the work of

your hand—in the fruit of your womb, and the offspring of your livestock, and the produce of your soil—for good. For *Adonai* will again rejoice over you for good, as He rejoiced over your fathers—

when you listen to the voice of *Adonai* your God, to keep His *mitzvot* and His statutes that are written in this scroll of the *Torah*, when you turn to *Adonai* your God with all your heart and with all your soul.

"I call the heavens and the earth to witness about you today, that I have set before you life and death, the blessing and the curse. Therefore choose life so that you and your descendants may live,

by loving *Adonai* your God, listening to His voice, and clinging to Him. For He is your life and the length of your days, that you may dwell on the land that *Adonai* swore to your fathers—to Abraham, to Isaac and to Jacob—to give them.

EKKLESIA:

Matthew 16:18-19: *And I also tell you that you are Peter, and upon this rock I will build My (Ekklesia) community; and the gates of Sheol will not overpower it.*

I will give you the keys of the kingdom of heaven. Whatever you forbid on earth will have been forbidden in heaven and what you permit on earth will have been permitted in heaven."

PRAYER:

Matthew 6:9-15: And when you are praying, do not babble on and on like the pagans; for they think they will be heard because of their many words.

Do not be like them, for your Father knows what you need before you ask Him.

"Therefore, pray in this way: 'Our Father in heaven, sanctified be Your name.

Your kingdom come, Your will be done on earth as it is in heaven.

Give us this day our daily bread.

And forgive us our debts as we also have forgiven our debtors.

And lead us not into temptation, but deliver us from the evil one.'

"For if you forgive others their transgressions, your heavenly Father will also forgive you.

But if you do not forgive others, neither will your Father forgive your transgressions.

Matthew 7:7-8: Ask, and it shall be given to you. Seek, and you shall find. Knock, and it shall be opened to you.

For everyone who asks receives, and the one who seeks finds, and to the one who knocks it shall be opened.

Matthew 21:22: And whatever you ask in prayer, trusting, you shall receive.

Psalm 23: A psalm of David. *Adonai* is my shepherd, I shall not want.

He makes me lie down in green pastures. He leads me beside still waters.

He restores my soul. He guides me in paths of righteousness for His Name's sake.

Even though I walk through the valley of the shadow of death, I will fear no evil, for You are with me: Your rod and Your staff comfort me.

You prepare a table before me in the presence of my enemies. You have anointed my head with oil, my cup overflows.

Surely goodness and mercy will follow me all the days of my life, and I will dwell in the House of *Adonai* forever.

About the Author

Rolland Wright is the Founder and President of First Place Ministries, home to the Choose Life Journal and Ekklesia Hub. His hunger for the Word and passion for Ekklesia drive this ministry. Discipleship and embracing our identity in Yeshua are foremost in his writings. He is an alumnus from Biola University.

Photo:
Courtesy of Rafael Estrada

www.ingramcontent.com/pod-product-compliance
Lightning Source LLC
Chambersburg PA
CBHW082104140626
46553CB00018B/636